D1508156

Capitalism Comes to the Backcountry

This book is about space, about language, and
about death; it is about the act of seeing, the gaze.

Michel Foucault, *The Birth of the Clinic* (1973), ix.

Capitalism Comes to the Backcountry
The Goodyear Invasion of Napanee

Bryan D. Palmer

between the lines

Published by:
Between The Lines
720 Bathurst Street, Suite 404
Toronto, Ontario
M5S 2R4
Canada

Cover and interior design by Goodness Graphics
Cover photograph by Neil Ward

Printed in Canada

This edition not for sale in the United States.

Between The Lines gratefully acknowledges the financial support of
the Canada Council, the Ontario Arts Council, the Ministry of Canadian Heritage,
and the Ontario Ministry of Culture, Tourism, and Recreation.

Canadian Cataloguing in Publication Data

Palmer, Bryan D., 1951-
  Capitalism comes to the backcountry: the Goodyear invasion of Napanee

ISBN 0-921284-86-1 (bound)   ISBN 0-921284-87-X (pbk.)

1. Goodyear Canada Inc.   2. Business relocation – Ontario – Napanee.
3. Tire industry – Ontario – Napanee.   4. Industrial relations – Ontario –
Napanee.   I. Title.

HD9161.5.T574G67   1994   338.7'67832'0971359
                                         C94-932095-1

MAIN

For Dorothy and Edward Thompson,
Residents of the backcountry,
Citizens of the world

Contents

Preface

This is a book about capitalism in motion, about how a major multinational enterprise, Goodyear Tire and Rubber Corporation, established a new plant in a small town. The town could be anywhere in Canada or the United States, anywhere, that is, where unions are weak and jobs needed and cherished, where people, politics, property, and priorities can be moved to accommodate power. A lot of places fit this particular bill. The older core of traditional blue-collar, smokestack-industry North America is disintegrating, its once peripheral backwaters assuming a new importance as the cartography of political economy in the late twentieth century is redrawn.

Napanee, Ontario, happened to be the right spot at the right time. Especially helpful was its geographical location, in what was once the heart of industrial Canada, nicely situated in terms of North American automobile production and tire consumption. This prime location was complemented by other, more human, factors. It is one of those locales seldom actually named by a burgeoning literature on global economic restructuring, plant relocations, workplace closings, new methods of "flexible," "just-in-time" production, and fashionable managerial conceptions of "team"-oriented output. What happened to Napanee as Goodyear worked its magic promise of jobs was nothing less than an act of colonization, a kind of cultural imperialism. This story, a narrative of speculation and spectacle, educational and state compliance, unfolds in the pages that follow against the backdrop of international financial wheelings and dealings. At stake were billions of dollars and the closing down of a unionized factory. As Goodyear incorporated Napanee into its global corporate empire, accomplishing this before a single tire was trucked out of its ultramodern plant, the town tilted in particular directions.

Acknowledgements

It is fitting that this book owes much to people and little to the largesse of institutions, corporations, and granting agencies. Queen's University, through its Advisory Research Committee, provided me with a small grant of $700 that allowed me to copy some documents, travel to Toronto, and reproduce photographs. I thank the Committee. Shelley Aylesworth-Spink of Goodyear helped me with a few phone conversations and a letter, and provided me with one or two helpful items. But for the most part Goodyear wants no part of any inquiry into its business. The company routinely turns down requests for interviews, plant tours, access to company publications, and anything akin to privileged/confidential information.

My real debts are to friends Adam Givertz and Marcus Klee, who kept prodding me to do this study; they were supportive to the enthusiastic extreme. Neighbours in Newburgh talked to me about the early rumours, about the Napanee high school and its seemingly corporate agenda, and about Goodyear's interview process. They kept me posted, and they kept me interested. Neil Ward showed me how to see with his exquisite photographs, while Nick Rogers, who also used his camera on my behalf, listened to accounts of Goodyear many times. I first met Susan Meurer in the Mine Mill and Smelter Workers' hall in Sudbury. Our paths crossed accidentally, but when I learned of her involvement with the Etobicoke plant closing and she heard of my interest in the Napanee story, she became a valued resource. She shared materials and her own artistic productions with me selflessly, and she wrote me detailed letters that became important pieces of documentary evidence.

Carole Condé and Karl Beveridge were also encouraging and generous; some of their work with the Communications and Electrical Workers of Canada is reproduced here. Paulette Peirol, of *The Whig Standard* (Kingston), and photographer David Smiley were gracious with their help. David W.T. Matheson took time away from a busy schedule to provide me with a helpful reading of the entire manuscript. The discussion of the Etobicoke plant closing could not have been written without the active contribution of David Birrell, President of Local 232, United Rubber, Cork, Linoleum and Plastic Workers of America, who gave me access to the local union's impressive files and a series of photographs. Donald Swartz of Carleton University helped me track down a source. I am especially grateful to Mark Arsenault, who provided me with a unique perspective, and to all others who agreed to be interviewed or provided permission to reproduce illustrative material. The people at Between the Lines were always a pleasure to work with.

Permissions

For permission to reprint various photographs and other illustrative material I am grateful to: Edward Regan and *The Globe and Mail*; Neil Ward; Doubleday, New York for Figure 7, adapted from P.W. Litchfields's *Industrial Voyage* (1954); Carol Condé, Karl Beveridge, and the Communications and Electrical Workers of Canada; Harvey Schachter and *The Whig-Standard*; Nicholas Rogers; David Birrell and Local 232, United Rubber Workers of America (Etobicoke); Susan Meurer; *Etobicoke Life*; David Smiley; B. Spremo and *The Toronto Star*; Ross Lees and *Napanee Beaver*, *Weekly Guide* (Napanee).

Chronology of Events

Most of this account of the Goodyear invasion of Napanee concerns events that happened within a few years in the late 1980s. Often the text turns on shifting developments within a few days. Almost always, its focus is on themes and issues that predate the actual building of the Goodyear factory, although those themes bear a relationship to the ongoing productive history of Goodyear Napanee. I thus isolate strands of the story, work with them, and then pick up other strands. In the end the pieces are meant to be understood on their own terms; but I also hope that, placed alongside one another, their cumulative character will reveal something of the scope and dimension of Goodyear's effort and accomplishment, an exercise in capital's primitive accumulation of hegemony.

1854   Napanee incorporated as a village

1898   Goodyear Tire and Rubber Company established in Akron, Ohio

1900   Paul W. Litchfield hired as plant superintendent, Akron

1910   Goodyear enters Canada, opening a plant at Bowmanville

1917   Goodyear builds New Toronto/Etobicoke plant

1919   Creation of Industrial Assembly

1936   Congress of Industrial Organizations sit-down strikes, Akron

1942   Certification of United Rubber, Cork, Linoleum and Plastics Workers of America, Local 232, Etobicoke

1986   Early November, Goldsmith hostile takeover bid

1987   May, closing of Etobicoke Goodyear factory

1987   August, rumours of multinational locating in Napanee

1987   Early December, property accumulation apparently thwarted with refusal of Milligans to sell family farm

1987   December 11, NDSS student rally

1988   March 25, official Goodyear announcement to build Napanee plant

1988	May-June, state aid re remission duties is announced
1988	July 13, Napanee-Goodyear Friendship Festival
1988	NDSS Project THINK; FIRE Program
1988	September, land speculation reaches peak
1988	September 23, building tradesmen picket plant site
1988	November, Goodyear hires first 60 maintenance workers
1989	January, construction of plant well under way, foundations laid
1989	January 31, Polydore St. Jean, USWA member, suffers fall at plant construction site, later dies
1989	April 1, NDSS processes 2,500 applications for 400 jobs
1990	January 25, first tire rolls off Goodyear line
1990	June 25, totally autonomous production
1993	Full production capacity reached; 15,000 tires daily

A Billboard in My Backyard

Neil Ward

It is the summer of 1992. For weeks eastern Ontario has been drenched with rain and covered with clouds, but for a couple of days there have actually been clear skies. People are smiling again. Around one in the morning, after spending a few hours in a local watering hole, I am driving my familiar route from downtown Napanee to nearby Newburgh. The sky is alight with stars, the moon full, suspended on the horizon like some surrealist sphere plucked off the set of Warren Beatty's *Dick Tracy*. I moved to Newburgh eight years earlier and had never imagined night skies this beautiful, the sparkling clarity breathtaking in its simple artistry.

Now, as I drive along the Palace Road, the darkness above my head-lights broken only by natural light, my eyes are drawn north to an unnatural glow. Rising above the landscape, across the distance of farmers' fields, is an industrial structure, box-like in its piled-up terminal point, multi-storeys high, shrinking to a more elongated kilometre-long extension that rises again at the far end. Obscured by trees and summer foliage, the building is a massive intrusion, spatially and architecturally, into an ecosystem and constructed environment of barns, winding country roads, fences, woodlots, and rural dwellings. It is night-shad-owed by its lighting system, which projects the plant's presence upwards, where it is visible (from some angles for miles) to motorists cutting a swath through rural southeastern Ontario en route to or from Toronto on the region's major transportation artery, the 401 or Macdonald-Cartier Freeway.

This is how Goodyear sometimes "looks" to residents of the Napanee area: an image of incorporation glowing on the evening horizon, a shimmering afterthought tucked out of daytime sight, but irrepressible in the clear dark of night. This is a piece of the city (jobs, economic security, profit) come to the country. Jimmy Reed's distinctive blues vocals, typified by a four-bar beat and walking bass line, often come to mind as the Goodyear skyline breaks through the still dark of an eastern Ontario night:

> *Bright lights, big city*
> *Gone to my baby's head*
> *Bright lights, big city*
> *Gone to my baby's head*
> *I tried to tell the woman*
> *But she didn't believe a word I said.*

Himself a migrant from the Mississippi countryside to the foundries of Gary, Indiana, Reed could employ the metaphor of gendered innocence as he experienced the rough transition to the class exploitation and power realities of modern capitalism:

> *Big boss man*
> *Can't you hear me when I call*
> *Well you ain't so big*
> *You just tall that's all.*[1]

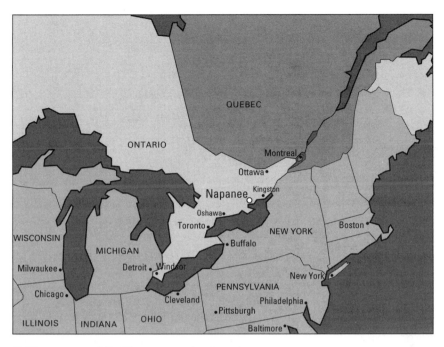

■ **Napanee and its (tire-consuming) environs**

For more than three years I have been pondering the Goodyear plant and its coming to Napanee, threatening to write something that would explore such matters, an essay unlike the dry treatises so common in academic life. As my eyes adjust to the hazy image of the sprawling structure of the tire company's linear buildings, I decide that I will indeed get down to work on such a project. And then my mind wanders, my eyes drift back to the road, and I imagine scenes from a few years before, when tire dumps at St. Amable, Quebec, and Hagersville, Ontario, went up in sooty, acrid, black smoke, creating a nationwide alert to what was obviously a potential environmental disaster. The clean-up left provincial governments with millions of dollars in bills.

Some twenty-six million passenger tire equivalents are discarded in Canada every year. They are unloaded in landfills, burned, stockpiled, recycled, exported to the United States, and utilized as fuel in the cement industry. Some are actually used to form underwater tire reefs, which supposedly attract and enhance possibilities for marine life, or to make floating protective breakwaters that shield marinas and shorelines from storms. (What it means to dump tires in ocean or lake waters and

E. Regan/ *Globe & Mail*

■ Hagersville Tire Fire

leave them there is a question that comes to my mind, but others seem unconcerned.)[2] But these tires are mainly an ecological nightmare. In the words of George Gaudet, an inspector with Prince Edward Island's Department of the Environment, tires "come back to haunt you."[3]

Now tires are being produced around the corner, by a company that will soon be pumping out fifteen thousand of them daily. I live in the backyard of the world's most modern tire plant. Yet the actual Goodyear factory is hidden: it is not really meant to be seen, and tours and tourists are not allowed; you can travel the back roads to a designated lookout sight, but you cannot easily get a peek inside the actual edifice of radial tire production. David Harrison, the Akron-based manager of Goodyear plant public relations, explained in 1988: "The tire industry is an extremely proprietary business. The president of the corporation is the only one authorized to sign the consent forms you have to visit a given plant on a given day. I've worked for Goodyear for 20 years, and even I need permission from head office to visit a plant."[4]

The boundaries separating the physical (as opposed to ideological) Goodyear from its neighbours are, and have been from the first stages of construction, well defined, as indicated in an early corporate preoccupation with security. It is an irony worth noting that for all of its promotional playing up of the familial relationship of Goodyear as a company and Napanee as a "community," this kinship is restricted to particular realms. Behind the actual walls of production, apparently, lie private properties that are unlikely to pay public corporate dividends. This is a familialism decidedly nuclear, a household shouting out news of its wholesome integration into the wider world of "community" at the same time that it guards this incorporation in ways that keep a great deal "closed."

For much of the Napanee region, the image of Goodyear impressed on this hegemonic field of vision has been the corporation's "advertisements for itself." The most sustained component of this campaign has been a huge billboard placed strategically distant from the 401. Proclaiming Napanee to be "Home of the World's Most Modern Tire Plant," the highway placard appeared to millions of motorists as a fleeting statement of corporate presence and community identity: a glimpse of the essentials was what the billboard was meant to convey.

Scrutinized in context, with its symbolism — internal and external — read analytically as expressive of particular social relations, the company's construction of its own field of vision widens out into unintended

■ **Security, I: Stop**

■ **Security, II: Danger**

meanings. The corporate symbol, the Goodyear Blimp, penetrates, phallic-like, the willowy calligraphy announcing the town. Set incongruously upon ground used for grazing, the billboard rises triumphantly above the countryside, which appears prostrate and decayed, the rotting remnants of a long-deceased tree providing a rare break in the monotony of the languid landscape. Life in the backcountry is reduced to its most animalistic, trapped between the brutality of enclosure (barbed wire) and the technology of modern management—a phenomenon that controls not only the earth, but also the heavens.[5]

Chapter Two

Concepts and Context: Democratic Aesthetics and the Imagery of Incorporation

Neil Ward

Capitalism does not so much come to the countryside. The backcountry is itself the site of historical transformation, generating social (gender/class) relations, protoindustrialization, demographic convulsions, and market forms pivotal in the transition to capitalism.[1] So this book's title is something of a misnomer. The title would seem to posit an opposition between, on the one hand, capitalism as a full-blown economic order and, on the other, the backcountry, a rural enclave of structures and sentiments somehow pristine in its freedoms from the impersonalities of the cash nexus, the exploitation of labour measured by the wage, and property privatized so as to shatter the hold of moral economies and customary practices of tenure and use. But that opposition is most emphatically not what I want to convey.[2] In the history of the white settler societies that make up much of English-speaking North America's past, this urban capitalist/rural pastoral divide is the stuff of mythology, speaking largely in the language of ideology and illusion.

Yet I want to retain this perception and argument about movement — forceful movement at that — for reasons that will become apparent as I describe how a large corporate concern recently established itself in the countryside of eastern Ontario, near the central Canadian town of Napanee.

This is, for many, a small part of a much larger story. Capitalism is engaged in a spatial restructuring that has critical consequences in terms of the global and regional dynamics of corporate location and relocation; this, in turn, is often viewed as directly related to a quest for more "flexible" forms of labour process specialization and accumulation, which, correspondingly, are linked to national industrial policies promoted by governments of a decidedly "right" tilt.[3]

Unionism, with its historic ties to particular kinds of industrial communities, finds itself weathering an especially bad storm in the last decades of this twentieth-century shift in capitalism's boundaries. Traditionalist understandings of the respective "places" of labour and capital appear to be disintegrating as "all fixed, fast-frozen relations, with their train of ancient and venerable prejudices and opinions are swept away," and "all that is solid melts into air."[4] The contemporary crisis of advanced capitalism's North American labour organizations has been depicted as a function of the sinking of the Fordist "community" (where blue collars and relatively high rates of unionization, consumption, and wages prevailed for much of the 1945-75 period), a once-secure ship now awash in the turbulent seas of plant shutdowns and runaway shops.[5] Gordon Clark, for instance, argues that the collapse of trade unionism "can be traced, in part, to unions' dependence upon inter-community solidarity, a fragile democratic ideal which is often overwhelmed by economic imperatives operating at higher scales in other places."[6]

These are matters of considerable practical and interpretive importance, but I want to sidestep them. My concerns here are not of this sort, however important they may be, and whatever their intricate relationship to my own subject. Instead, I want to address what is often ignored in the abstracted big picture of capitalism's contemporary restructuring. This is a study of "the manufacturing of consent," an examination of just how, in a context of specific human needs, capital manages to extend its needs into the realm of universal need, to bury its own interests in an avalanche of "benevolence," highlighting not the inequities of social relationships but their supposed reciprocities. Goodyear's invasion of Napanee, to be sure, was courted and pleaded for by the subjects and future subjects of its subordination — to the point that voices of resistance were all but silenced — but it was no less an act of colonization for all that. There are no ties that bind as effectively as those that are self-imposed, those that appear in the historical record of oppression and exploitation at the request of the very people they will secure. "Domination has its own aesthetics," wrote Herbert Marcuse, "and democratic domination has its democratic aesthetics."[7] What follows is an exploration of the "democratic aesthetics" of capitalist domination.

This exploration, and that democratic aesthetics, commenced, as my night-time drive by the Goodyear plant and my gaze at the corporate billboard suggest, with what may seem to some a decidedly unmaterialistic and meandering pastiche of sights. But it is sight itself, with its myriad materialist consequences, that is the subject of this account. My purpose is to present a moment of contemporary history as it was visualized by (or, perhaps, presented to) those who lived it, and then to "read" that vision against its constructed purposes. The act of seeing dominates the modern era, as writers such as Richard Rorty, Michel Foucault, and Guy Debord stress; but as Martin Jay suggests, this "scopic regime of modernity may best be understood as a contested terrain, rather than a harmoniously integrated complex of visual theories and practices."[8] The Canadian environmental philosopher Neil Evernden notes: "Vision permits us the luxurious delusion of being neutral observers with the ability to manipulate a distant environment.... The loss is any notion of interrelation between the elements of the visual field. We see only what is, not how it came to be." Jacqueline Rose, pointing in the same important interpretive direction, closes her book *Sexuality in the Field of Vision* with the words: "Our previous history is not the petrified block of a singular visual space, looked at obliquely, it can always be seen to contain its moments of unease."[9]

The images of incorporation I present in this book introduce yet more images. For the most part these are not images of struggle but of an almost "naturalistic" consensus, so firm in its hegemonic assumptions that the act of contestation easily seems marginalized to the point that it is out of sight and, consequently, out of mind. That accomplished, opposition is also apparently out of history. To reconsider these images, to look at them obliquely the better to appreciate the dimensions of unease that are necessary to reconstruct a practice of contest on the ground of incorporation, is to begin the material process of reappropriating the critical act of seeing. Capital, as the case of Goodyear coming to Napanee demonstrates strikingly, is extremely adept at presenting its "singular visual space," at "harmoniously" integrating visions that contain — in both senses of the word — fundamental conflict. This book is about other ways of seeing.[10]

Chapter Three

"Pre-History": Company and "Community"

Before the billboard announced capital's invasion, Goodyear as a company and Napanee as a "community" had their respective histories, which were and are not ones of equality.

Goodyear Tire and Rubber Company began as a modest operation launched by Frank A. Seiberling, who took advantage of the depressed economic context of the late 1890s to purchase from the Akron Woolen & Felt Company a seven-acre site with two dilapidated buildings and a power plant. With an initial outlay of only $13,500 spread over five years, Seiberling raised almost $100,000, drew on family knowledge of the rubber business, and parlayed his original production of bicycle and carriage tires into the age of the automobile.[1] Named after Charles Goodyear, whose 1839 discovery of the hot vulcanization of rubber earned him a unique, if financially unhelpful, deity status in the commercial rubber industry, the new corporation was geographically well situated to supply the auto plants of nearby Detroit and Cleveland. After an early bout with patent and other legal restrictions and campaigns, the Seiberling enterprise grew phenomenally. World War I, with its explosive need for tires and other rubber products (from gas masks and valves to balloons and airships) catapulted the firm into world prominence. Sales soared from $110 million in 1916-17 to $223 million in 1920; 30,000 Goodyear workers toiled in the Akron plants, and the city itself, riding the new rubber boom, exploded, its population climbing from roughly 70,000 in 1910 to 255,000 in 1929; a $10,000 investment gamble in Goodyear at the end of the 1890s would have been worth $1 million by 1920. The corporation was on its way to becoming an empire.[2]

Goodyear Tire and Rubber was not simply the creation of Frank Seiberling, his brother Charles, and their astutely chosen management "team," however much corporate histories would like to mythologize such creatively rugged entrepreneurial individualism. Rather, the firm rode the wave of the second industrial revolution with its new technologies, products, workforces, managerial innovations, and markets into the war years of booming profits.[3] But that wave was not without its disturbing dips, and in the recessionary downturn of 1921 the company faced the threat of receivership. The era of the Seiberling family control came to a close as the firm was reorganized and refinanced under the direction of a new corporate board of directors, with cash infusions from Cleveland banking interests. Goodyear thus survived the difficult years of adjustment associated with the postwar reconstruction period, cut back its labour force, doubled productivity per worker, and more than halved the average cost of labour per hundred pounds of output. By the end of the 1920s the company was not only the world's largest tire producer, it was also the largest rubber enterprise. Employing over forty thousand workers, it sold its products in 145 countries, controlling rubber plantations in Costa Rica, Sumatra, and the Philippines and establishing plants in Canada (Bowmanville, 1910; New Toronto-Etobicoke, 1917; St. Hyacinthe, 1926), Australia, and England.

Goodyear survived the Great Depression of the 1930s and was quickly integrated into wartime production needs in the 1940s. "The Goodyear Spirit was never more evident than in these most troubled times," concludes a seventy-fifth-anniversary Canadian company history. Goodyear continued to expand on a world scale in the post-1945 years. By the early 1980s corporate sales totalled $9 billion annually, employees numbered 132,000, and 101 manufacturing facilities were operative in twenty-eight countries. Ranked in the top forty of *Fortune* magazine's five hundred largest U.S. industrial companies, Goodyear's postwar growth took place in the traditional tire production sector, but the company expanded to tap other markets as well. Aerospace and military items figured centrally in this diversification, but the company also produced and promoted a wide range of domestic consumer goods and services, including rubber snow-removal blades employed in airports. In Canada Goodyear was involved in supplying the wheel, brake, and tire assemblies for the ill-fated AVRO Arrow, ostensibly the world's fastest fighter aircraft, but a plane that never went into production. Goodyear also developed steel-cable conveyor belting for use in various industries and resource extraction processes, including coal and potash mines from the Soviet Union to northern Alberta. As the company prepared to establish its base of operations in Napanee, Goodyear Canada Incorporated, 89 per cent owned by the Akron parent, boasted sales of just under $700 million, eight large manufacturing plants, hundreds of service centres and retreading plants, as well as a surprising array of secondary product facilities. In the late 1980s, with a workforce of five thousand, Goodyear Canada had an annual payroll of just under $200 million.[5]

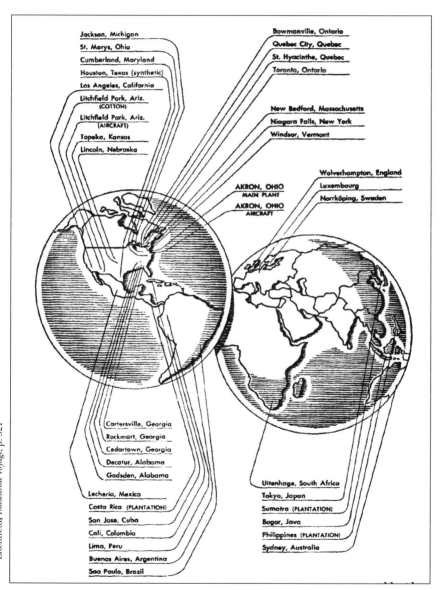

Litchfield, *Industrial Voyage*, p. 321

Jackson, Michigan
St. Marys, Ohio
Cumberland, Maryland
Houston, Texas (synthetic)
Los Angeles, California
Litchfield Park, Ariz. (COTTON)
Litchfield Park, Ariz. (AIRCRAFT)
Topeka, Kansas
Lincoln, Nebraska

Bowmanville, Ontario
Quebec City, Quebec
St. Hyacinthe, Quebec
Toronto, Ontario

New Bedford, Massachusetts
Niagara Falls, New York
Windsor, Vermont

AKRON, OHIO MAIN PLANT
AKRON, OHIO AIRCRAFT

Wolverhampton, England
Luxembourg
Norrköping, Sweden

Cartersville, Georgia
Rockmart, Georgia
Cedartown, Georgia
Decatur, Alabama
Gadsden, Alabama
Lecheria, Mexico
Costa Rica (PLANTATION)
San Jose, Cuba
Cali, Colombia
Lima, Peru
Buenos Aires, Argentina
Sao Paulo, Brazil

Uitenhage, South Africa
Tokyo, Japan
Sumatra (PLANTATION)
Bogor, Java
Philippines (PLANTATION)
Sydney, Australia

■ **The globe according to Goodyear (1954)**

There is thus no denying the magnitude of the corporate presence that would eye the Napanee region in the late 1980s. This was a capitalist giant with global reach. It was also associated with a specific ideological stand. A steadfast opposition to unionism was couched in a purposeful blend of "Americanism" that congealed patriotism and the politics of committed anti-Bolshevism in institutionalized efforts to construct an "industrial republic." Striding alongside this, at times, rather abstract and heady mix of ideals and illusions was an elaborate corporate familialism that encompassed gendered bonding through physical and sporting activities, employee representation plans and awards, and an early and wide-ranging company commitment to innovative welfare programs.

Early in the company's history a baseball team was formed. "Many of the men on the team had, or soon attained, the rank of foreman," one Goodyear executive remembered. "And when a factory worker, acting as umpire, could call his boss out in a close decision at third base and make it stick, it helped to create good relations." This truly was a case in which winning or losing was secondary, and how you played the game was of utmost concern. From baseball Goodyear graduated to "group and factory-wide picnics, fish fries, sleigh-ride parties, and occasional dances," all of them dutifully attended by an owner, Charlie Seiberling. In 1918 a company-sponsored basketball team won the American Industrial Athletic Association championship, and Goodyear Hall's gymnasium was the site of intra-company competitions throughout the 1920s. From the 1930s to the 1950s, Goodyear's "Wingfoots" competed successfully in various basketball bodies and tournaments, including the National Basketball League, amateur forerunner of the National Basketball Association. Squad members often competed at the Olympic level, winning gold medals. By the 1960s Goodyear had become internationally known for its extensive and award-winning employee recreation programs, which included, besides basketball, bowling, golf, tennis, fishing, hunting, riflery, flying, model railroading, volleyball, soccer, baseball, softball, and, in Great Britain, cricket.[6] The family that played together, Goodyear's leading executives obviously thought, stayed together.

"Family spirit," as Goodyear's official historian Hugh Allen noted in 1949, was also fostered through the company's Labor Department. In an effort to retain the closeness of the family firm in the face of the expanding impersonality of modern labour relations, Akron-based Goodyear established a 1909 Relief Association, a voluntary society providing for employees who fell sick or suffered a debilitating accident; opened a factory restaurant and hospital in 1912; established a newspaper, *The Wingfoot Clan*, as a communications bridge between workers and management; built a landscaped 112-acre company subdivision (Goodyear Heights) providing workers with accessible housing and a large athletic facility (Seiberling Field); linked the local Boy Scout operation to Goodyear, which built lodges, boasted five troops headed by foremen and other staff, and rewarded "outstanding" boy scouts with motor trips and outings to a northern Canadian retreat at Lake Temagami; broke new managerial ground with the creation of a 1913 salaried Flying Squadron composed of workmen who were deliberately trained in diverse areas of all departments so that they could attend to any difficulties that developed across the entire spectrum of mass-production activity; offered courses at a Goodyear Industrial University, which by 1920 focused on business-related subjects such as bookkeeping, typing, shorthand, public speaking, credit, and personnel relations and eased immigrant workers into an "Americanization" program through language classes; rewarded long service, productivity, and worker co-operation and ideas with pins, medals, and cash bonuses; and, in a year of acute class struggle, 1919, instituted the Goodyear Industrial Assembly, which was modelled on the U.S. Constitution and provided for employee representation; as well as joining with Goodrich, Firestone, and other Akron employers to bankroll a Home Owners Investment Company that facilitated the building of almost five hundred houses.

In Goodyear's Canadian plants the Flying Squadron graduated its first member in 1919, and as of World War II the company was sufficiently established to accentuate its importance as an intrinsic part of the national economy, producing goods "manufactured in Canada ... by Canadian workers ... for the Canadian marketplace." Complementing this promotional nationalism was the "family" foundation of the Canadian plants: "Goodyear already had fathers and sons, brothers and sisters, uncles and nephews working in Bowmanville, New Toronto and St. Hyacinthe—starting a long tradition of their families becoming a part of the Goodyear family ... bringing their spirit in as part of the Goodyear 'Spirit.'"[7]

Behind much of this conscious program of familialism and harmonizing class interests was the human centrepiece of the Goodyear empire, Paul W. Litchfield. Hired by Seiberling in 1900 as the Akron plant superintendent, Litchfield was a graduate of the Massachusetts Institute of Technology. He would survive the 1921 corporate reorganization, spending fifty years as a Goodyear director and thirty as chief executive officer, charting the company's course of expansion throughout the Third World and into a number of industrial-capitalist nations, Canada included. Indeed, Litchfield combined business trips to Canada with fishing and camping expeditions and the purchase of a camp site at Lake Temagami. Litchfield took prospective company leaders to the camp, testing their self-reliance and introducing them into his inner circle. There, too, he integrated the post-1921 crop of officers from banking and financial backgrounds, sealing Goodyear loyalty with the rituals of uninhibited masculinity.

> I cannot think offhand of anyone in all these years who was a good camper who did not also prove to be a good man for the company. And men who camp together come to know each other better, work better together afterwards.... If anyone feels free to sneak up behind you and drop a cold slimy fish down your back, you are on a different basis with him than by merely talking to him in the office.... Temagami has become almost part of the company's training program. I suppose every executive is always subconsciously screening the younger men coming into the company, trying to pick out future leaders. So for many years now we have been sending promising young men from the Squadron or the colleges up there for ten days or two weeks with some of the older executives, sometimes two or more groups. At the last count Temagami had 420 alumni.[8]

Litchfield stamped this robust hands-on managerial orientation into class relations at Goodyear. In the production of tires and other products he saw at work the grand philosophies of Americanism, individualism, and familialist "productive pride." At odds with this layered world view were communism and the so-called "new" unionism.

In the opening pages to his 1920 book, *The Industrial Republic*, Litchfield saw the main threat to a peaceful world order in Russian Bolshevism, with its "anarchistic" and "autocratic" call for "the destruction of all capital," ideas premised on "ignorance" and leading to "idleness and starvation" for "over a hundred million people of the white race."

Bolshevism is an industrial disease, and a very contagious one wherever it finds lack of confidence in the management of industry, or a feeling of injustice amongst working-men with their present conditions. The problem which we must solve is to find a remedy for stopping the spread of Bolshevism. The first step toward this solution is a careful study and examination of the industrial situation, ferreting out any injustice which may be present, and establishing a feeling of confidence between the working-man and the management of industry.

For Litchfield, then, "Management and government are synonymous terms, one being usually applied to the political and the other to the industrial world." These worlds came together in the American republican ideal, which Litchfield insisted required an educated mass citizenry and "a community of interest amongst the people, and the absence of sharply drawn class distinctions." Litchfield thus blended a managerial commitment to "discipline and efficiency" with a responsibility "for fair play and fair treatment." Following Henry Ford, he reduced the hours of labour to eight, and in 1916 he implemented paid vacation time and a pension plan; other Akron capitalists supposedly deplored his radical ideas, which they caricatured as "socialistic."[9]

But Litchfield was no socialist. He despised and feared Bolshevism, and saw radical unionism and working-class struggle as its domestic counterpart. Deeply shaken by a 1913 Akron strike led by the Industrial Workers of the World, Litchfield recalled the conflict as "an attempt on the part of a left-wing group to seize power." It was a dangerous sign of the capacity of the mass production worker to succumb to "the forces of mass psychology." As the Wobblies flooded Akron with leaflets declaring "A Message from Hell" and "Less booze for the bosses! More bread for the workers!" mass picketing shut down the city's major rubber plants and the strikers' ranks ballooned from 3,500 to 14,000 over the course of three days. According to Litchfield, "Mobs of men wearing red badges were patrolling the streets and terrorizing the populace," a perilous state of affairs that justified a reign of vigilante repression in which God and Country were invoked to induce the strikers to return to their jobs. Shortly after the Wobblies went down to a crushing defeat in Akron, 125 Goodyear employees in a raincoat division had the temerity to walk out. Litchfield climbed up on a table and with a perfunctory exclamation — "You people don't want to work"— spontaneously fired the lot.[10]

The 1913 I.W.W. strike left Litchfield concerned with the "underlying unrest in the face of the growing mechanization of industry, something a radical group could appeal to and capitalize on, intimidating other workers by force and violence, as had happened in the strike." The wide-ranging program of welfare measures at Goodyear and the creation of the Industrial Assembly, described by Litchfield as "the keystone of our whole labor program," were meant to siphon such discontent and fore-stall a slide into overt class struggle. The timing of Litchfield's creation of the Flying Squadron in 1913, although not solely attributable to labour strife, was not unrelated to the work stoppage of the same year and the presence of Wobbly organizers in Akron.[11] As one of the most sophisticated employee representation plans in existence within U.S. industry, the Goodyear Industrial Assembly simultaneously Americanized immigrant workers (to participate, workers had to be U.S. citizens and understand the English language), provided for the resolu-tion of shop-floor grievances, and integrated capital and labour in a har-monious illusion of shared power.[12]

Voting "citizens" of the factory were known as "Industrians," and they met in a dignified assembly, in bodies known as the Senate (composed of older employees with longer service records, men expected to pro-vide a "sober second thought") and the House of Representatives. Elected working-class delegates, under the watchful gaze of the Stars and Stripes and the company flag, could address any and all matters of concern to the employees, including wages. But if their proposals went too far, as they did in a 1926 demand for a 12.5 per cent wage increase, either Litchfield himself, as the factory manager, or the board of direc-tors had final veto power.

Throughout the 1920s Goodyear's consciously constructed self-image and Litchfield's guiding personnel relations maxim were devotion "to the building of men instead of the building of machines." In a 1920 publication, *Work of the Labor Division*, Goodyear expounded its "indus-trial philosophy": "Nothing touching the lives and best interest of Goodyearites is a matter of indifference to Goodyear. Here is the expla-nation of the boundless enthusiasm, kindly atmosphere, and spirit of co-operation which built up the many plied, trouble resistant structure of Goodyear success. Goodyear has all about her the human quality. And it has been to this human quality fully as much as to her business methods, that Goodyear owes her meteoric rise in the ranks of

American Industry."[13] Litchfield saw the Industrial Assembly as the linchpin of a successful stint of labour-management co-operation reaching from its founding through the 1920s and into the mid-1930s, when he claimed it was legally terminated by the Wagner Act's provisions outlawing collective bargaining procedures funded by employers.[14]

In fact, the denouement of the Industrial Assembly, though not unrelated to the New Deal's foray into establishing a regime of industrial legality, was more directly a consequence of a mid-1930s upturn in class conflict. American Federation of Labor efforts to crack Goodyear in the 1933–35 period produced some organizational breakthroughs, but nothing to reverse the long-standing company policy of dealing with its workers through its Industrial Assembly representation plan and treating union delegates as individuals. Handcuffed by its insistence on isolating rubberworkers into sectionalized craft jurisdictions, the AFL stalled and sputtered in Akron, souring the name of unionism among workers who grew disdainful of organizers complaining that the disgruntled operatives expected "the moon on a platter all in a month."

Organizational opportunities revived late in 1935. Goodyear had implemented an intensified six-hour day to soften the depression-blows of unemployment and lay-offs, but now seemed poised to reintroduce longer hours of labour, sustain the pace of work, and cut piece rates, all without consideration of the workers recently laid off. Despite almost universal opposition to this corporate direction among Goodyear employees, Litchfield, who would "disestablish" the body in 1937, turned decisively away from his long-standing reliance on the Industrial Assembly's representational ideal. According to testimony before the LaFollette Committee Hearings, members of the Flying Squadron were trained in the use of tear gas and munitions throughout 1935 and 1936. Workplace "democracy," under the pressure of class struggle, gave way to corporate autocracy.

In the face of rising resentment among the rubber workers, sit-down strikes erupted at Goodyear throughout January and February 1936. Soon the AFL was pushed aside, and rubberworkers aligned with the more militant and dynamic Congress of Industrial Organizations union, the United Rubber Workers of America, later renamed the United Rubber, Cork, Linoleum and Plastic Workers of America (URW). But for the most part job actions were spontaneous, and only after a massive month-long walkout was well under way in February did the CIO union formally recognize the strike as its own. Perhaps lessons learned in the Industrial Assembly translated into the organizational coherence of the 1936 struggle, which saw mass picketing of Goodyear's eleven-mile perimeter, the erection of three hundred tarpaper shacks to keep the strikers warm, armed mass resistance to a sheriff-led attempt to reopen the struck plants, and a radio-orchestrated campaign to beat back the threat of 5,200 organized vigilantes.

For its part, Goodyear stood pat. Eight days into the strike Litchfield declared that he would offer no concessions to mob violence: "As a citizen of this community and as the head of this corporation, I cannot be a party to any recognition of the theory that government stability has collapsed and that the seat of constituted authority has been forcibly removed from the city hall and the courthouse to the center of the mob that mills before our gates."

Settled in late March, the strike was a victory for the rubberworkers, but the company was adamant that it would not sign any agreement or recognize the union as sole bargaining agent for the workforce. A rash of sit-down strikes erupted in the months following the settlement, and it took eight years of sustained conflict to produce something of a resolution. Goodyear finally recognized the presence of the United Rubber Workers in its Akron plants in 1944.[15]

The Goodyear Industrial Assembly had been vanquished. Litchfield saw its passing as a consequence of the intrusion of the Roosevelt New Deal on the freedom of the individual, and he lamented the rise of a unionism in which communists figured as agents of an effort to "*overthrow ... our government.*"

American workmen are probably more stable than those of other countries, but the communists traded shrewdly on their decent human impulse to stick with their fellows—and they were adroit in using the forces of mass psychology. Their real purpose was of course completely hidden. We should not criticize workingmen for failing to realize what that purpose was. Thousands of well-meaning people in all ranks of society accepted and passed on as truth the poisoned half-truths of communistic propaganda without realizing they were being used as tools. The hostility toward business, which they stigmatized as capitalism, had the same source.... A number of these unions, but not all, recognized the danger and threw these men out. But I do not believe any-one is naive enough to believe that the communists gave up after that, got out of the labor movement. There are too many indications of the small hard core of communist minorities still there, influences not interested in *any* settlement but in prolonging the quarrel and stirring up new disorders, outlaw strikes, outbursts of violence, continuance of industrial war.[16]

Industrial Valley, Ruth McKenney's 1939 account of the turbulent events in Akron in the mid-1930s, saw the passing of the Industrial Assembly differently. When it rejected Litchfield's order to return to the eight-hour day, the "company union bit the hand that fed it," and a few days later the "oldest and best-known company union in America was done to death ... at the hand of its founder." From that point on "the Goodyear Industrial Republic" was little more than "a pathetic ghost."[17]

McKenney analytically buried the body of a company union, but the ideas and premises of Goodyear's Litchfieldian industrial republicanism lived on. Translated into many foreign languages and transposed to set-tings throughout the world, the Goodyear managerial style adapted to the changed context of the late twentieth century. Work artists Carole Condé and Karl Beveridge depict the meaning of contemporary corpo-rate familialism in their staged photographic collage of the motifs of the new domesticity of capital. While babies in hard hats are objectified as engines of consumption, children's toys project the new entrepreneur-ial commitment to encouragement rather than discipline. Yet the power behind the new scenes of worker placation is ever present, controlling and manipulating labour for the old ends of profit and ownership. Litchfield's program of familialist incarceration, which Condé and Beveridge could easily adapt to their generalized image of "the corpo-rate family," would figure as an important integrating force in Goodyear's eventual invasion of the small eastern Ontario town of Napanee.[18]

In the last decades of the eighteenth century, the demographic dislo-cations of the American Revolution produced a mass migration of United Empire Loyalists into the Aboriginal lands of what is now south-eastern Ontario. Many of these white settlers occupied plots adjacent to Lake Ontario's Bay of Quinte and took up farming. Six miles inland, Native peoples had long acknowledged an impressive river site, known

Carol Condé & Karl Beveridge in collaboration with the Communications & Electrical Workers of Canada

THE CORPORATE FAMILY

■ The Corporate Family

as the Appanea Falls. In 1785-86 a grist mill was constructed to serve local farmers. The mill was later purchased by a Kingston Loyalist merchant, Richard Cartright, who by the mid-1790s had expanded the operations to include a tavern, distillery, sawmill, and wool processing mill. With the 1830s and 1840s came modest economic expansion, a town survey, and the sale of lots. In 1854, with a population approaching two thousand, Napanee was incorporated as a village. The arrival of the Grand Trunk Railway in 1856 solidified the village prominence in the region, and in short order Napanee, a distinctly British town, beat back other contenders to become the seat of government for Lennox and Addington County, securing in the process a county courthouse, jail, and registry office. Napanee's population had climbed to five thousand by 1895.[19]

Well-known as a flour-producing site whose Victorian riverside industries catered to local and, in the case of Gibbard's furniture factory, national markets, Napanee peaked in this late nineteenth-century period. As larger firms concentrated in central Canada's more populous and heavily industrialized Golden Horseshoe region (from Oshawa to Niagara Falls), for Napanee the first half of the twentieth century was a time of population stagnation and even slight decline. No significant mass-production industries located in the town, which by mid-century sustained a series of medium-sized employers, including Gibbard's, Nabisco, Air Shade Aluminum, and Pet Milk, few of them boasting payrolls of over one hundred employees. Between 1906 and 1955 the population of Napanee dipped slightly, falling from 4,300 to 4,000. Thereafter it rose marginally, reaching 4,500 in 1966. By the time Goodyear was contemplating Napanee as a potential new location in the late 1980s, the town population stood at 4,900.[20]

Unionism would eventually secure a toehold in the region, and in the aftermath of World War II labour bodies such as the United Automobile Workers made sporadic efforts to organize local strongholds of the open shop, such as Gibbard's. But the town largely escaped the acrimonious clash of contending class interests. As early as 1864 the *Napanee Standard* paid homage to one mercantile pillar of the village, the first warden, John Stevenson. His praises were sung in words conveying well the hold of paternalism and pride in capitalist accomplishment:

> *Thy stores are thronged like some o'erloaded hive,*
> *Where nestling bees in constant labours thrive,*
> *Void of that pride and aristocracy*
> *That mars some fame, but not thine, Napanee.*
> *Among the host of thy industrious men,*
> *Not least does one claim notice from my pen;*

Stevenson's name, it rings on many an ear,
Creating hope, and oft dispensing fear –
His funds engaged the workmen's hands to employ,
To banish debts and cause the poor to joy.
Thy beauteous home thus nestling on yon hill,
Could charm my harp and all its music fill.
That joy I leave to the sweet birds of heaven –
That chant their song with powers that God hath given.[21]

As Napanee experienced the labour mobilization of the Knights of Labor in the 1880s, 185 members affiliating with Courage Local Assembly 9216, the Order's local organizer wrote Terence V. Powderly to complain of the climate of intimidation that kept the working class in check. "This section of the country is sadly in need of organization," Thomas J. O'Neil concluded, "but fear of the money kings (the Rathbuns) keep the working class in slavery."[22] As late as the mid-1960s only four of sixteen major Napanee and district employers were unionized. The Napanee Industrial Committee took some pride in reporting that the town had practically no history of "labour disturbances"; labour turnover was minimal and efficiency "extremely high." All of this was attributed to "good management-labour relations."[23]

Skitch Studios, Napanee / Photogelatine Engraving, Ottawa

■ **Napanee, aerial view, 1940s**

Photogelatine Engraving, Ottawa

■ **Napanee, Dundas Street, 1940s**

Cordial class relations may well have been characteristic of Napanee in the late twentieth century. But, by 1985, after more than a decade of recessionary downturns, the obvious pressing need was not so much class harmony as access to work. Official annual unemployment statistics for the Economic Area 5–10, which includes the county of Lennox and Addington and the town of Napanee, fluctuated between 7 and 9 per cent in the 1985–89 period, rising to 10.1 per cent in 1991. Seasonal rates could top 13.5 per cent, as they did in March and April 1992. In 1988 towns such as Napanee, and eastern Ontario in general, were routinely depicted as "chronically depressed" in comparison to Ontario as a whole (read: the Golden Horseshoe). *The Financial Post*, covering Goodyear's coming to Napanee with a full-page article, noted, "It was no accident that a giant multinational chose to locate in this town of 4,900, where unemployment sits at 7%–8%, above the expected provincial rate of 5.1% for 1988."[24]

Napanee's mayor made the case bluntly: "Napanee wants Goodyear. We need the jobs as well as the obvious spin-off of other industries. We want to grow and provide jobs for our children. Those jobs are gone. Now at least some are back. Toronto can afford to share some of its bounty.... That city's unemployment is the lowest in the province; ours is the highest."

Unemployed youth needed the kind of incentives Goodyear would provide, moving them out of the summer employment/winter UIC syndrome. "If Goodyear can provide work I'll be at the head of the line," one jobless nineteen-year-old said. "I've got a tent. I'll even camp out to be the first ... if they have steady jobs." Without Goodyear, said a disgruntled seventeen-year-old, "there's no future here."[25]

Goodyear's invasion of Napanee was indeed no accident. It was a finely tuned orchestration of clandestine reconnaissance and shrewd dealings with and manipulation of local forces and needs, capped by a final, ostentatious bread and circuses blowout. Goodyear drew on its own corporate traditions to ensure a situation in which its coming to Napanee would be celebrated rather than contested; it managed this end exquisitely.

Chapter Four

"Cloak and Dagger" Beginnings:
The Price of Property

In August 1987 rumours circulated in Napanee about a large multinational corporation that was thinking of locating in the area. Jack McNamee, the town's clerk-administrator, received a letter from a Toronto lawyer representing an unnamed company that was looking to build a new plant. The lawyer asked for specific economic information about the region and indicated that the company was also considering a number of other sites, twenty-six in all — making it clear to town officials that something of a competition for this new enterprise was on. McNamee decided not to courier the information, but instead drove the 240 kilometres to Toronto, dropped in on the lawyer, and had "a nice talk."

McNamee and Jim Kimmett, a clerk and industrial commissioner for Richmond Township (an adjoining administrative unit just north of Napanee, where Goodyear would eventually build), followed up this initial personal contact with further meetings and more data. Two representatives of the mystery company showed up in town in November. According to McNamee, they were "laid-back guys" who spoke with "a bit of an accent."

Talk in town was that the new corporate settler could be any number of things: a refrigeration-equipment maker, Carrier Corporation of New York, a West German conglomerate, or a U.S. automaker. Those betting long shots speculated that Jim and Tammy Faye Bakker were going to build a born-again Christian fantasyland. After the company men made it clear that they would back out of any deals if the name of their firm was discovered and revealed, regional officials were not inclined to investigate the company's identity. The company executives apparently wanted to keep the price of property low, and were also concerned about the possibility of adverse publicity if they ended up bailing out of the project.

The unknown visitors walked the essentially scrub land of marginal farms, and over the course of the following months they met with local politicians and school board trustees, conferred with pivotal businessmen and bankers, and initiated discussions with suppliers of key services such as Ontario Hydro. No last names were exchanged. Goodyear executives later joked that when they came to Napanee they discarded all watches and tie-bars that bore the winged-foot insignia of the company. The only thing known about them was that they were Americans. Land sites were surveyed and rezoning applications made. Most importantly, options to buy hundreds of acres of property were secured. "It was cloak and dagger," the Napanee mayor, Harold Webster, commented. "Those fellows would come in here and talk things over but never let you know who they were. Theories were flying all over this place."[1]

Goodyear was obviously under pressure to build and modernize. Tire manufacturers had allowed plants of seventy-year vintage to lapse into technological obsolescence, and in the late 1980s both Goodyear and Firestone were closing the doors of factories established in the populous market centres of Hamilton and Toronto in the World War I years and after. Some 2,800 tire workers lost their jobs, including the core union workers in the rubber industry at the plant in Etobicoke, a large industrial suburb on the western edge of Toronto. Then followed the shutdowns of General Tire in Barrie, Ontario, and one of the Uniroyal-Goodrich plants in Kitchener, Ontario, resulting in 1,800 more unemployed. In Kitchener a 1988 United Rubber Workers strike flared into violence when the union refused the company's demand for a productivity clause. A truck loaded with tires was destroyed by a Molotov cocktail, three trailers were torched, a hundred police officers called in to quiet the situation, and twenty-seven workers arrested.

To Ontario's industry minister, Monte Kwinter, these plant closures and class conflicts were merely part of the global restructuring of industry. Company spokespersons, however, often used terms such as "cut-throat competition." Workers spoke with more venom. "I'm extremely angry ... it's just sickening," said David Birrell, president of United Rubber Workers Etobicoke Local 232.

For their part, Goodyear executives saw the matter as a case of strategic financial necessities in an age of predatory international capitalism. With the Japanese-controlled Bridgestone bidding to take over Firestone, the French tire concern Michelin biding its time for a successful absorption of Bridgestone, and a campaign looming against Goodyear waged by corporate raider Sir James Goldsmith, the Akron rubber giant was caught in a vice of declining productive capacity, new market opportunities, and worldwide competitive pressures, all of this exacerbated by a serious cash shortage. After losing $22 million in 1986, Goodyear Canada was facing further years of rising costs at its "marginal" operations. Opting to take immediate losses, rebuild, and reorganize, Goodyear Canada dropped a further $42.3 million over the course of three years (1989–91). The parent U.S. corporation lost $90 million in the first quarter of 1991, although it earned $65 million in the same period a year later. All of this was clearly foreseen in 1987-88 by Goodyear's directors, who also saw that they needed a new operation somewhere in Ontario. By 1990 the Napanee plant would be hailed as the "lead dog" in the Goodyear team, displacing a facility at Lawton, Oklahoma. Business commentator Dunnery Best referred to Napanee as "a winner in one of the most brutal epics of downsizing and bloodletting that an overcapacity industrialized world has endured."[2]

In December 1987, after months of clandestine reconnaissance of the local human and geographic terrain, this was all an unknown future development, and the elaborately constructed/concealed property coup appeared to be coming to a grinding halt. Rights to ten lots had been secured, but this was apparently not enough. Standing in the way of Goodyear's capacity to accumulate the property package it claimed it needed was a lone family farm, whose owner refused to be enticed by the anonymous company's agents and their offers of big money (said to be ten times market value) and confusing contractual obligations.

Ironically enough, Mildred Milligan, registered owner of 113 acres that would reportedly make or break the unnamed company's interest in Napanee, was the daughter-in-law of developer-friendly Clarence Milligan, former town councillor and Member of Parliament. In *They're Putting Us Off the Map*, a National Film Board movie made in the late 1960s detailing Napanee's demographic and industrial decline, Milligan moaned about not understanding "why industries don't come here, since the land is so cheap." When the Milligans refused to let their property go for offers that reputedly reached $800,000, the full weight of local officialdom was mobilized. Jim Kimmett of Richmond Township now joined forces with a Toronto real estate agent, the duo serving as the unknown company's negotiating team. But the Milligans were put off by the buyer's insistence on secrecy, and they pondered why the plant was to be located in a wooded area. They objected to the corporate insistence that their land would only be a "buffer zone," and its staunch refusal to indicate exactly where the new factory would be built. They strongly resisted a clause belatedly altering a leaseback arrangement in ways that gave the company a thirty-day vacate order capacity.

These objections were met with a deluge of pressure: all nine town council members and the reeve, or effective head of the local municipal council, tried to move Mildred Milligan off her resistance; her members of the provincial and federal parliaments approached her on the subject of the sale; even her father-in-law was enlisted in the cause to dissuade her. "You couldn't break her," town politician Harold Webster reported, and his sentiment was echoed by MP Bill Vankoughnet. Mildred Milligan reported that they all tried "every gimmick in the book" to convince her to sell. "They even went so far as to talk to my minister," she said. It seems the sense of "community" was unravelling as the price of property, and its many costs, went up.[3]

"We're being made out to be the bad guys with the black hats," Mildred Milligan's son Wayne said. Indeed, the family was subjected to an avalanche of rhetorical excess. McNamee exclaimed, "It was the guarantee of the future of the whole area, and our children's futures, and their children's futures. And it's gone." Kimmett was "really afraid Napanee and the whole area's name is going to be blackballed among these consulting people for generations to come." And yet still no one knew what company they were dealing with. Both McNamee and Kimmett acknowledged that their only contact with the entrepreneurial mystery men was through telephoning Toronto law and consulting firms and waiting for call-backs.

"If it's all so vital, if it's all so important, why hasn't there been even one little [company] official come down here to see us?" asked Wayne Milligan.[4] Indeed, the Milligans would not sell, but eventually a land package would nevertheless be assembled that would more than serve Goodyear's property needs. In the end the issue of land was not the only problem to be resolved, as future events would make clear. More than a lot was clearly at stake.

Just how much was up for grabs would be apparent in the months and years to come. The ultimate announcement of Goodyear's Napanee intentions, in late March 1988, triggered a speculative boom in the local

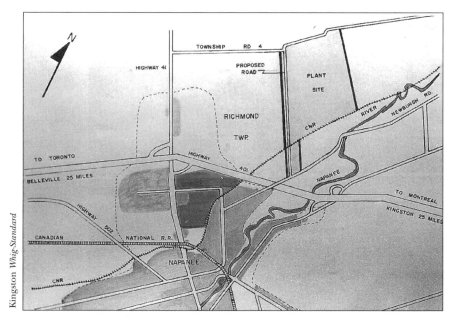

■ **Proposed Goodyear Plant Site**

real estate market. Public attention focused on rising housing prices, condominium developments, and brisk sales in residential lots, all related to prophetic pronouncements that the area's population was about to double, or at least expand by 2,500, with a subsequent need for four or five hundred new homes. Future Mayor Chris Seeley commented, "The initial excitement was tremendous. I don't think anybody was untouched by it. We heard predictions that Napanee would triple [in population] in two years."

Adrian Van Asseldonk, manager of the Napanee branch of the federal Employment and Immigration centre, speculated that between 1,400 and 4,600 spin-off jobs could materialize by 1994. Local real estate agents reported prices tripling and office staffs doubling. A major subdivision east of Napanee's industrial park was in the making, while Richmond Township farmland sold wildly in the most volatile market. On the south bank of the Napanee River a $20-million, sixty-three-unit condominium project known as Vyas Villa saw prices rise $5,000 in a day. The land had been on the market for twenty years. Would-be buyers were lured with free champagne and a string quartet, only to be informed that forty of the units had already been sold. One local realtor

Photos: Kingston *Whig-Standard*

■ **Vyas Villa Condominium Construction**

■ **South Shore, Napanee River**

described the situation as "out of control." For a few weeks, he noted, "when the town was full of three piece suits and attache cases, you just couldn't keep up."[5]

The biggest speculative game in town, and the truly large investment money, were in undeveloped farmland with close proximity to the proposed plant site. Farms bought for $40,000 two to three years earlier were drawing prices over $300,000. Local developers were "flipping" property in days; rumours circulated of hundreds of thousands of dollars being "made" in mere weeks. At the centre of one of the largest "deals" were Richmond Township official Jim Kimmett and Richmond Reeve Gary Hartin. Representing the township that had been so centrally involved in helping Goodyear assemble its property package, they sold an option to buy a fourteen-acre parcel of farmland to a development company linked closely to a Napanee law firm; one shareholder of the company was a Napanee town councillor who would later run for mayor. Ten days later the development company flipped the parcel, selling out to a numbered Ontario company. The first transaction carried a price of $350,000; the second a sales tag of $800,000: in less than two weeks $450,000 in profit had materialized, and unserviced land originally bought by the township at $3,000 an acre had soared by over 1,800 per cent in "value." Kimmett, who responded to inquiries about the land transactions by saying that "it was nobody's business what the township got" for the land, received a 2 per cent commission on the sale, but both he and Hartin were somewhat evasive about the ultimate selling price and the final buyer, who turned out to be a high-rolling Toronto wheeler-dealer, Stephen Mernick.

Moving into the Napanee region in a big way, Mernick was dealing in undeveloped local acreage in the same way that most people buy groceries. Reputed to be worth $50 million personally, with a portfolio of $700 million, and fresh from his acquisitive conquests of the $115-million Heritage USA site in South Carolina and the defunct Firestone Canada, Incorporated, tire plant in Hamilton (at a fire-sale price of $60 million), Mernick purchased a sixty-acre tract in the Napanee area for $1.5 million, upping a two-month-old purchase price by $500,000.

Mernick had managed to set up his numbered company in March 1988, about a week before it was disclosed that Goodyear would be coming to Napanee. He promptly contacted a Belleville engineering consulting firm to report on the feasibility of development. The company registered eleven real estate transactions within five miles of the Goodyear site on one Friday in September 1988, putting it out about $7 million; but it secured a hefty $11 million in mortgages at the Toronto office of the Bank of Montreal. There was much talk of hotel developments and industrial parks, with Mernick announcing his intention of purchasing some nine hundred acres of local land. He described Hartin and Kimmett as "phenomenal" individuals.

Another Toronto development firm called the Royal Group proposed building a $10-million, 130,000-square-foot shopping mall directly adjacent to the already established Napanee Mall. Noises were made about previous industrial sites being purchased, the buildings demolished, and the showcase commercial centre being set up by late 1989. Smaller strip malls went up; new businesses opened.

Less than three years later Mernick had reneged on many of his mortgages and was facing bankruptcy, owing the Bank of Montreal and the Bank Leumi Le-Israel (Canada) over $7 million. There was no new megamall in Napanee, many storefronts sported "For Lease" signs, and smaller strip malls stood virtually empty.[6] Local lawyers wondered aloud about how Mernick had managed to hoodwink the financial institutions: "These [bank] loans look to be the most foolish loans of the century," one of them commented. "This man just walks in and walks away with phenomenal amounts." The price of property and the men who made it in Napanee: "phenomenal" was indeed the word that fits.

■ **The speculative bubble burst (1993), I:**
Industrial land near Goodyear site remains unsold.

Nicholas Rogers

■ The speculative bubble burst (1993), II:
Small strip malls stand empty

The Mernick inflationary miracle, and its sordid deflation a few years later, exposed the extent to which the frenzied speculation and predictions of economic transformation of 1987-88 would prove overblown. Spinoff industries and developments did happen: machine shops were set up later in the shadow of Goodyear to service its specific needs, and projected development projects included a thirty-two-lane bowling alley.[7] But the impact of Goodyear's arrival, dated with the 1990 beginning of actual tire production, never did measure up to anywhere near the heights suggested by local boosterism. A kind of "industrial fever" nevertheless kept Napanee and nearby municipalities "hot" with development and speculation for some time after the initial 1987 rumours and the eventual announcement of corporate intentions in 1988. Throughout 1988-89 there were further rumours of industrial relocations, some supposedly involving multinational corporate giants and upwards of a thousand jobs, about to bless Napanee and the nearby towns of Belleville and Trenton. It was the Goodyear story all over again, with secret negotiations and unnamed firms.

Belleville's industrial director, Dave Parker, described the now familiar process of corporate reconnaissance: "Many of these industries deal with consultants who do not release the names of their clients. They work out of Toronto and come in and ask questions, look around and tell us they'll get back to us. We might not hear anything back for months, and even then we don't know who we're dealing with."

Richmond's Jim Kimmett, an old pro at the cloak and dagger meanderings of the company mystery train of relocation, proved particularly closed-mouthed when word leaked in late spring 1989 that the Napanee area was again being considered as a possible site for yet another major employer. "There are always five or six of them (companies) shopping," he said, and he worried that publicity would only "scare them off." Local officials had come to liken their situations "to the confidential nature of a priest in a confessional."

Sears Canada did establish its catalogue distribution facility in Belleville, but no major industrial producer followed in Goodyear's original stealthy footsteps.[8] In fact, as Goodyear's payroll climbed to 550 in the spring of 1993, the town's second largest employer, Emerson Electric, closed its doors. Emerson left almost 350 facing unemployment.

The material impact of this corporate invasion and the related rumour-mill of the bonanza to follow unleashed a scramble for political control of the spoils of development, as well as the first stirrings of discontent. The Napanee town council attempted a "land grab" in September 1988, instituting procedures that it hoped would culminate in annexation of choice parts of Richmond and North Fredericksburgh townships. Threatened with losing one-third of their tax bases and the lucrative centrepiece of assessment, the Goodyear plant itself, local officials in Richmond and North Fredericksburgh at first expressed shocked offence. One of them wondered about "what role, if any, Goodyear has played in the machination of this thing?" With 1992 prop-

Nicholas Rogers

■ Job creation/job loss:
Napanee's Emerson Electric closed down, 1993

erty and business taxes of $1 million, Goodyear would eventually pay the corporate equivalent of five hundred homes, and officials had long been clear about the extensive revenues and responsibilities that rested on the tire company's presence in the area. At issue was Napanee's role in servicing Goodyear and its proximate industrial developments, when tax revenues went entirely to other townships. Particularly troubling was the matter of water and sewer services, which needed new facilities and extensive upgrading, projected to cost millions of dollars.

Well aware of the difficulties that arose when Honda established a plant in Tecumseth township two miles outside the town of Alliston, Ontario, which had to provide the industrial employer with costly public utility and firefighting services, local political figures cooled down and began considering prospects of annexation and/or amalgamation. The contending local states looked for guidance to the larger provincial body, and Nevin McDiarmid, chief boundary negotiator for the Ministry of Municipal Affairs, remarked, "Things are happening at an awful clip out there, so we [the ministry] feel we have to look at this thing right away." A seven-member steering committee composed of elected officials from each of the three municipalities as well as their clerks (including old Goodyear allies McNamee and Kimmett) was struck to look into annexation. On the brink of an election, the key players, Richmond and Napanee, secretly signed an agreement in principle to amalgamate the two municipalities, a move criticized as a "shotgun wedding." The amalgamation was later rescinded by Richmond.

In Richmond Township, protests against a drive to

Nicholas Rogers

■ **A road for Goodyear**

rezone a local quarry so additional gravel could be crushed for the building of a road leading to the Goodyear plant led to considerable acrimony. A stormy public outcry won a court injunction prohibiting blasting at the quarry; Richmond officials were assailed with cries of "You're selling us off to Goodyear." At the same time Napanee residents met to oppose the rezoning of a thirty-acre development lot, claiming that the proposed residential subdivision would be designated as "low cost subsidized housing" that would lower property values in the vicinity.[9]

A number of Richmond and Camden East residents began to question the impact that Goodyear would have on the environment, particularly the preservation of water sources and the production of wastes. After months of unease they were tired of the "pat answers" and perpetual air of secrecy.[10] But given the vitriolic public nature of the assault on the Milligan family's refusal to sell their land to Goodyear, few citizens wanted to openly challenge the corporate goose that so many were counting on to lay golden eggs. When Goodyear held a drop-in promotional session on April 15, 1988, and Richmond Township residents were given thirty-five days to file objections to the firm's petition to rezone the land it held options on, no one came forward to object.[11]

For some residents of the Napanee community, then, the cloak and dagger beginnings of Goodyear's invasion were a problem. But the rising price of property tended to sweep resistance aside. When criticisms of Goodyear began to emerge from Napanee's rival, Kingston — especially in a *Whig-Standard* editorial with the title, "The Goodyear Shuffle"— local boosterism raised its voice. Napanee's mayor, H.W. Webster, extolled the firm as a responsible and welcome addition to the community. Editorials in the *Napanee Beaver* put out the royal welcome mat for the new industrial employer, and "Welcome Goodyear" signs proliferated throughout the town.[12]

Praise was heaped on Jack McNamee and Jim Kimmett, who cleared the way for Goodyear's second (and more public) coming. In December 1987, when the irksome Milligan family refusal to sell their land threatened to end the prospects of the mystery firm coming to Napanee, Kimmett and McNamee scrambled to find other acreage for the much sought-after employer to option. After securing what they thought was a reasonable alternative lot, they were devastated to find out that the company's interest in Napanee had cooled considerably. McNamee was reportedly told: "It's obvious you don't want us. We don't want to come in here under a cloud of controversy." The supposedly public relations-conscious company clearly had deep pockets, but exceedingly thin skin.[13] It needed to be stroked by the kind of youthful enthusiasm that aging bureaucratic alchemists and priest-like confidants such as Kimmett and McNamee, however zealous, could not quite muster.

Chapter Five

Enter Education: Student Power and the Napanee District Secondary School

Just as the land deals pivotal to Goodyear's coming to Napanee seemed about to collapse in December 1987, a segment of the town's youth centred in the Napanee District Secondary School (NDSS) jumped into the fray. Encouraged by the high-school principal, Rod Hughes, who had been following the secret company's negotiations from the early stages, the Student Council met with McNamee to hear about what was at stake: jobs.

A guidance counsellor at the school stressed that 65 per cent of the institution's graduates went directly into the workforce, and Hughes publicly stated that 80 per cent of the 260 students finishing their educations each year ended up moving to cities as far away as Oshawa and Ottawa to secure employment. Many students apparently began to take somewhat personally the pre-Christmas news of the failure to seal the multimillion-dollar industrial development proposal. They knew about the anger directed at the Milligan family for refusing to option its farm, and rumours had it that some of the local population wanted to organize a public protest rally at the Milligan homestead. One of the Milligan family reported that even the children of landowners who had agreed to sell were being "hassled" by students, and he feared that his own grandchildren would become "targets of harassment." "I never realized there were such sickies in our community," he said, "putting one kid against another."[1]

On December 11, morning classes at NDSS were delayed as the school's 1,470 students gathered in the gymnasium. Organized by the Student Council, who invited the media to attend, the assembly was depicted by the press as something of an angry wake. Speakers deplored the loss of local employment opportunities that would force the town's youth to leave the comfortable surroundings of their birthplace. Much

Nicholas Rogers

■ **Napanee District Secondary School**

would later be made of the virtues of locality and the alienating impersonality of distant labour markets. Student Council president Mark
Arsenault urged all students to write letters of concern to the town
council. "These jobs could have been for us," he said. "We must ensure
that we don't allow an opportunity like this to slip by again. People
think that Napanee is a hick town, and this only reinforces that view. We
need industry, since there are no jobs in Napanee."

Another student, Julie Foster, stressed the need to participate in the
letter-writing campaign, "so that the community knows that we care, and
that we tried." These views were endorsed by the school staff and by
District 52 of the Ontario Secondary School Teachers' Federation.
Local teachers' union president David Allison described the Milligans'
refusal to sell their land as a "disappointing Christmas present." He told
the students, "This is the biggest news to hit Napanee in the 13 years
I've been here. But it's the wrong kind of news." Videotaped by NDSS
technician Mike Murphy, the assembly was later aired on a local cable
TV station and shown to the town council.[2]

This was student power of a unique kind. The assembly would come
to be described as a "corporate pep rally." To see the videotaped proceedings, however, is to appreciate how "unpeppy" the whole understated event was. But it was the very idea of the student assembly, which

soon reached mythic proportions in its stature in the local area, that was central. And the supposed job-hungry "spirit"— largely an ideological construct of local media and development boosters — proved an impressive selling point.

Jack McNamee made sure that the somewhat disgruntled unknown company got a copy of the student video. Months later, when Goodyear's decision to establish a Napanee plant was finally announced, Akron spokesmen claimed that their interest in the town was restored by seeing the tape of the student rally. In March 1988 Stan Mihelick, executive vice-president of Goodyear U.S., made NDSS one of his first stops, and he was full of praise for the students. "We looked at a lot of places in Ontario," he said. "I had been favoring Napanee, but I was having difficulty selling it to my bosses. But what you people did was the key.... That tape was the thing that convinced us that Napanee was the right place to put it." Goodyear Canada president Scott Buzby, proclaiming "Napanee's never going to be the same," saw NDSS as the company's chief drawing card: "You can just feel the energy, the enthusiasm and the fine education of these students. It was the high school that carried the day." The company was "all so impressed" by the tape and "the wonderful job" the students did.

The *Napanee Beaver* was effusive in its praise of student activism: "Those kids at the high school did something that not every teenager would do in this day and age — they actively involved themselves in their community. They saw an opportunity and then seized it.... that tape did the trick, because the top Goodyear brass in Akron, Ohio, certainly took notice."

Principal Rod Hughes seemed to be in his element. He said that in Goodyear's own words, NDSS was "the top school" the company had come across when it came to programming. "Their key decision in locating here is the match between the education system and their potential needs." In fact, Hughes spoke almost as long at the "student" assembly as council president Arsenault, laying great emphasis on the high school's importance as a training ground for industrial citizens. NDSS technical director Barney O'Connor concurred. "When we were designing the program we designed it with this in mind," he said. "We designed for the future of modern industry." Indeed, years later, in 1993, NDSS would be featured prominently on the CBC-TV program *Venture*, in a story about the new economy of "brains and education." In the 1990s, *Venture* claimed, fitting local educational systems to the needs of corporations has replaced tax breaks, land gifts, and direct investment as the major incentive used to attract corporations to specific regions.

Arsenault proposed following up the high-school success story with a telegram to Goodyear thanking it for its efforts and signed by the entire student body. More impressive was a huge tire, constructed and signed by the students and presented to Buzby. Arsenault later recalled with a laugh that the gift was meant to symbolize that the first tire built in Napanee came out of NDSS.[3]

■ **Preaching to the converted: Stan Mihelick, executive vice-president, Goodyear Tire and Rubber, in Napanee.**

■ **NDSS students gather in gymnasium to hear Goodyear officials**

Strangely, the NDSS Student Council-led "information rally" that was turned into a strong youthful vote for corporate development and its promise of jobs might almost appear to be an inversion of 1960s student power. Decades earlier students stood *against* the establishment; at NDSS in 1987–88 they were apparently all for it. Moreover, their action was almost universally seen as a spontaneous expression of autonomous student opinion. Most NDSS student leaders probably believed all of this themselves during the time they were making television, radio, and front-page newspaper news.

From the vantage point of the early 1990s, a self-reflective Mark Arsenault has come to look at things somewhat differently. He now recalls the prompting and the quick pace with which everything came conveniently together. While careful to note that he has no proof of some of his suspicions, he finds it curious that NDSS principal Hughes figured so prominently in all the post-Goodyear announcement celebrations. Aware that the prophetic speculations of demographic growth, socio-economic transformation, and expanding job opportunities had come to virtually naught, Arsenault remembers the 1987-88 winter as one in which he and others were a convenient public relations peg upon which Goodyear's coming to Napanee could be quite successfully hung. He now sees that "The kids who I went to high school with aren't benefiting. I know one guy who got a job there."

How did the historic student assembly actually come to happen? Arsenault's recollection begins not with his own role as Student Council president, or with the role of fellow students. He says that most students, himself included, were "totally blind ... we didn't know what was going on." But apparently there were some people with better vision.

The entire Student Council was summoned to the office of Guidance Counsellor Terence Murray on a Thursday, in spite of the fact that Murray was not the regular faculty advisor. Murray informed the student leaders that an unknown firm looking to locate in Napanee was about to pull back for reasons associated with its failure to secure a required land package. He emphasized the jobs that would be lost and the potential growth that could be squandered. The students were urged to do something. Arsenault remembers distinctly that Murray wanted them to go home, make banners and placards, phone their friends, and then lead a 9:00 A.M. walkout protest at the school on Friday morning. Murray apparently craved militant action. But the guidance counsellor also advised them that the students should keep quiet about who had suggested the protest, warning them that it could not get out that they had been prodded to action by him. "As an employee of the Board of Education I was being mildly seditious," Murray recalls now, and at the time he felt his act of advising the students to protest should be "off the record." While some members of the Student Council reacted enthusiastically to Murray's ideas, Arsenault was more guarded in his response, and he scotched the idea of a walkout protest as impossible to organize on one night's notice. The local youth "are a pretty conservative lot," Murray says.

After that initial meeting, Napanee town councillor Jack McNamee was contacted by someone in a position of authority at NDSS, and he made time to see the students on very short notice and explain the situation to them. McNamee was pessimistic, believing that the corporate mystery train had been derailed, but he told the students to go ahead and do what they could. Arsenault and others approached Principal Hughes, asking him if they could schedule an emergency student assembly for nine o'clock the next morning. Not known for his ready accommodation of student requests, Hughes nevertheless immediately agreed to the assembly.

Amazingly, this whole process — convening, listening to Murray, discussing it among the Student Council members, seeing McNamee, finding Hughes agreeable to a morning assembly — took only a couple of hours. With the benefit of hindsight, Arsenault is now "confident that Hughes and Murray got together" and mapped out a strategy so that Hughes could not be seen to be manoeuvring the students. Murray himself denies this, although he acknowledges that the entire staff of NDSS had talked about the opportunities for jobs that were about to be lost should the much-sought-after mystery company not build in the Napanee area. He also notes that Hughes was deeply committed to training high-school students for the job market, that NDSS programs were corporate-oriented, and that in the future the principal would prove eminently adaptable to Goodyear's needs.

Whatever the *personal* intricacies of influence, suggestion, and overt manipulation, there is no denying that the Student Council did not so much act on its own praiseworthy initiative, as countless sources would later claim, but that it was amenable to the suggestive influence and congenial aid of NDSS faculty and administration. Arsenault went home to write the speech that would eventually be cited as the cause of

Goodyear coming to Napanee. The student president notes that at the assembly the next morning NDSS technician Mike Murphy was ready with his camera and videotape equipment, but he has no recollection of any student asking Murphy to record the proceedings. Most students still did not know what was happening, Arsenault suggests, adding that it was not even so much jobs that excited them, but the expansive cultural possibilities that many thought would follow Goodyear to town: movie theatres, recreation facilities, and the like.

But after his speech, and its quick videotaped transfer to Akron, Arsenault was at the centre of a whirlwind of publicity and special treatment: he was a guest of honour at a town council meeting and ate dinner with Hughes, Buzby, and Ontario premier David Peterson; he sat prominently on the stage during a Napanee-Goodyear Friendship Festival held on July 13; he went for a ride in the famous blimp; and Goodyear officials courted him with interest in his talents as a hockey player.

"They used me pretty well," Arsenault says. "I got nice things out of it. It was a good plan, if that is what it was. It worked for them — 90 per cent of the selling point was 'the students' and we made it look like this was right."

What remains in Arsenault's consciousness is a deep-seated suspicion that Goodyear was not in fact swayed by the students, but had already made up its corporate mind. The company constructed the imagery of student enthusiasm captivating Akron's head offices because it made good media copy and solidified community support for Goodyear. Hughes and Murray first led the students to believe that they mattered, and Goodyear followed this up by cultivating the importance of local youth to their relocation plans. Arsenault thinks it was all "a little too pat."[4]

However significant Arsenault's role, and whatever the impact of the student assembly and youthful goodwill, Goodyear and school officials had solidified a relationship early in the company's forays into eastern Ontario. Willis Boston, director of education for the Lennox and Addington County Board of Education, kept his eye on the unknown corporate visitors in the secretive first stages of land acquisition. Goodyear knew well the importance of tight local connections with small-town high schools through its experience in Lawton, Oklahoma, the site of Goodyear's flagship operation, and the company was no doubt attracted to the various programs that NDSS had sponsored over the years, many of which provided direct vocational and technical training or strove to create attitudes that most businesses would cherish. Such programs were promoted by the Napanee Industrial Committee in 1966, and in the late 1980s NDSS was involved in a co-operative Technical Advisory Vocational Committee composed of representatives from local organizations, employers, and unions. Throughout the 1980s NDSS established connections with major Ontario industries and institutions — among them General Motors, Ford, Chrysler, Dupont, Northern Telecom, and Queen's University — all of them donating millions of dollars of computer hardware, equipment, and parts to the school's industrial arts program.[5]

More telling was the introduction of PROJECT THINK into NDSS. Goodyear paid for Principal Rod Hughes and the school's technical director, Barney O'Connor, to travel to Lawton, where the duo viewed Goodyear's "team members" in productive action and toured the local high school. Hughes came back with a taste for how the Napanee school could adopt programs in place in the Oklahoma town, thereby integrating the school more effectively with the community's major corporate employer. Concerned that school image reflect purposeful education,

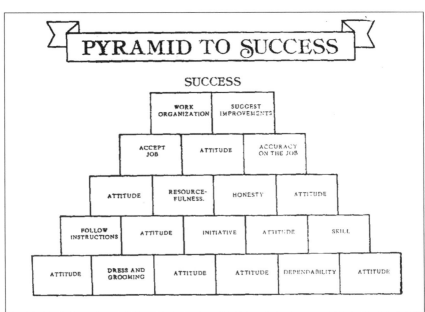

■ Pyramid to success

Hughes conceived of PROJECT THINK as a trigger, a way of making self-discipline work, as it supposedly did in Goodyear's Lawton plant, through an honours system prompted by simple word commands. If students or staff were saying or doing improper things, "Think" was to be used as a trigger word to remind offenders of their "responsibility to our

---

PROJECT THINK

CONCEPT:

Project Think is a system for empowering all people to control to some extent the school image.

HOW IT WORKS:

The word "Think" will be used as a trigger to remind us of our responsibility to our school image.

WHY USE THE WORD "THINK":

We are in the business of developing minds to have the right attitude, discipline and skill for future success. To think requires activity on the part of the learner - our job as teachers is to determine thinking capability and attempt to raise thinking to higher levels. This implies education.

As well THINK is used continually in most classes in a positive manner.

WHAT SHOULD HAPPEN:

Assume that students will be instructed through grade assemblies this Friday that staff will be using the Think Project approach with them starting Monday, January 9th.

EXAMPLE 1:   You notice a student drink pop in the hall. Use the Think Project approach and proceed as follows. Get the student's attention and say to the student THINK. (nothing more)

   If the student says what are you talking about, or what am I doing wrong, then take the student aside, talk to them in a calm controlled manner, and explain what the Think Project is all about, and why you used it in this case.

   If the student chooses to ignore you, proceed as above and counsel the student by taking them aside as above.

   If the student challenges you remain calm and in control, request that the student come with you, and bring them to the office.

   If the student will not come to the office, remain in the area and, if possible, get the student's name to be forwarded to the office and, if possible, send another student to the office for a V.P. or the Principal.

   In all cases of not following expectations, staff must act and must remain calm and in control.

EXAMPLE 2:   You are in the hall and observe one of your colleagues ignoring a student. You have the obligation to say to your colleague "THINK". However do no more than this unless your colleague asks why, then explain and leave it.

EXAMPLE 3:   You are in the staff room or in public and a colleague starts talking negatively about a student, other staff, program, etc. You say "THINK", and try to get the individual to state the problem and then be creative in dealing with it.

■ **Project Think**

school image." This would ostensibly develop young "minds to have the right attitude, discipline, and skill for future success," all of this seemingly constructed in ways and terms that related directly to employment and the labour market. An appendix to Hughes's PROJECT THINK outline depicted a pyramid to success based on attitude, personal presentation, dependability, skill, initiative, and the capacity to follow instructions, and peaking in job and work-related accomplishments.[6]

Hughes's gung-ho enthusiasm for Goodyear's methods drew minor criticisms from parents, and there was soon reference to renaming NDSS Goodyear Tech. One NDSS student in Grade 9 when Goodyear arrived on the Napanee scene recalls that Hughes was very much influenced by the company and remembers his job-oriented stress on teamwork and his assimilation of company practice into the high school's routine. Area residents questioned the extent to which job training for Goodyear was going to undercut programs such as music and languages, pointing out that after Goodyear's initial hiring stage — which would not likely take in many of the local students — there was not going to be that many jobs anyway. A *Whig-Standard* commentator asked, "How is it that Goodyear can recruit an entire high school to its cause while a social reform agency would be barred at the door, at worst, or admitted for a brief visit, at best?" He concluded that the answer was pretty obvious: jobs.

> It is not enough for Goodyear to be hiring from a random assortment of people knocking at their gate. They want a local pool of potential employees who have had the rough edge knocked off and are prepared to bestow their loyalty upon the company in return for decent pay and good working conditions. In the outcome, Goodyear will continue to manufacture good tires, make a profit, and hire more local people. That is the nature of the implicit contract behind the new management system being put in place at the Napanee Secondary School.[7]

PROJECT THINK had a short lifespan. According to a later NDSS principal, Mike Dollack, the strong "family ties" that Goodyear developed in its production facilities simply could not be reproduced in a high school.[8]

Whatever its brevity, PROJECT THINK signalled the willingness of local educational authorities to toe a particular corporate line. Moreover, if PROJECT THINK was too crudely derivative and obvious in its purpose of attitudinal corporate tracking, NDSS's more general, long-standing programs were sufficiently oriented to preparing students for employment that they satisfied most entrepreneurial needs. PROJECT FOCUS, for instance, provided for "aesthetic awareness" and the understanding of "theoretical principles," with advanced-level courses aiming to prepare students for university entrance. But the school's basic and general-level courses, which in 1989 Hughes saw as fundamental to the life trajectories of the majority of NDSS students, were designed to produce "employable citizens" capable of finding work in either "low-skill repetitive task" jobs or economic spheres requiring apprenticeship training or community-college level skills. In the words of one NDSS publication, students were in school as a way of "Learning a Living." They were there to "Learn to Earn." An NDSS "Monthly Attitude and Attendance Evaluation" reinforced this reality, laying stress on a student's attention to instruction, willingness to participate, punctuality, and responsibility.[9]

The most dramatic statement of NDSS's commitment to education as a kind of "work-ethic" training was a unique and somewhat controversial program known initially simply as FIRE. Meant to deal with students who repeatedly violated rules, refused to complete assignments, or otherwise failed to live up to the all-important expectations of achievement

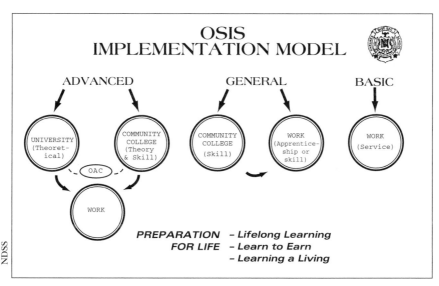

■ **Education as preparation for labour**

and attendance central to NDSS's consciously constructed self-image, FIRE was introduced by a preamble that left no doubts as to its meaning and intended impact:

A large percentage of the students, who leave Napanee District Secondary School, go directly to work. Many employers state that secondary school graduates, who gain employment with them, are not properly prepared to fulfill the expectations of the world of work. Punctuality, productivity and application to the job at hand seem to be

---

Napanee District Secondary School

245 Belleville Road
Napanee, Ontario
K7R 3M7

MONTHLY ATTITUDE AND ATTENDANCE EVALUATION
(MARKS FOR EXAMINATIONS AND TERM WORK NOT INCLUDED)

NAME OF STUDENT: _____   COURSE: _____

HOMEROOM: _____   MONTH: _____

TEACHER: _____

		MARK	SPECIFIC COMMENTS
1. Participates willingly	(0-2)		
2. Listens attentively and follows instructions	(0-2)		
3. Speaks politely and clearly	(0-2)		
4. Co-operates	(0-2)		
5. Completes tasks	(0-2)		
6. Treats others with courtesy and respect	(0-2)		
7. Brings necessary equipment	(0-2)		
8. Strives for excellence	(0-2)		
9. Arrives on time	(0-2)		
10. Attends regularly	(0-2)		
TOTAL	20	20	

NOTE: The mark will be recorded when this form is returned to the subject teacher with appropriate signatures.

Teacher's Signature _____

Student's Signature _____

Parent's / Guardian's Signature _____

Parental Comment: _____

Telephone: (613) 354-3381
378-6671

The Lennox and Addington County Board of Education

NDSS

■ **Attitude and attendance evaluation** (NDSS)

the areas in which secondary schools can do better when educating young people.

At N.D.S.S., we can do more for our graduates who plan to enter the work force. We must teach them that there are consequences when an employee fails to meet the expectations of the employer. Sometimes, employees are even fired!

Under the FIRE program, students sixteen years and older whose performances at NDSS were judged inadequate and/or disruptive could be placed on "a probation list." Teaching staff were expected to begin compiling a documentary record of a probationary student's shortcomings, with particular reference to areas designated by the specific words "attendance," "productivity," and "application." A committee screened the problematic record of such "candidates" for firing. If there was no improvement in the student's overall performance, the offending youth was brought before a panel composed of NDSS administrators and teachers as well as his or her parents/guardians. A "contract" was drawn up, binding the student to a particular set of rules and work routines that would ostensibly put the young productivity offender back on the road to social and academic success. If that contract was broken, "The student will be fired from his or her courses at N.D.S.S. for a stated period of time."

The process provided for appeals to the principal, but after being fired students were expected "to complete the exercises and assignments" in a booklet, "Home Instruction Regarding Employment." Any fired students who did not avail themselves of the opportunity of home improvement were to be given a copy of the NDSS brochure, "Final Instruction Regarding Employment." In Hughes's words, FIRE was a "future-oriented" program with an emphasis on the reality that most students will have to adapt to a work environment: NDSS prepares them for this with its "can do" attitude.[10]

The FIRE program was apparently a bit hard for the Lennox and Addington County Board of Education to swallow, but board members eventually coughed twice and sanctioned the unique experiment in teaching students that employers have rights and employees responsibilities. Before the implementation of the program, according to Hughes, NDSS had twenty to thirty problem students a year, with roughly half of them dropping out. After the introduction of FIRE, eighteen students came before the panel between September 1988 and February 1989, and only three ended up being lost to the system. Some four years later, with the program renamed HIRE/FIRE to accentuate the positive, NDSS principal Mike Dollack claimed that 67 per cent of the credits in

F. I. R. E.

Student's Name ....   Homeroom ....

Staff Member ....   Course ....

Date of Referral ....

Students 16 years of age and over may be processed through the F.I.R.E. Committee. Referring a student to this recourse is a very serious matter. DO NOT advise the student that you are taking this course of action. THE FIRE PROCESS IS A LAST RESORT. Before referral, consider the following:

ATTENDANCE PROBLEMS   Check appropriate boxes

Have you tried -   talking with the student?   ☐

                                   consulting with the homeroom teacher?   ☐

                                   consulting with the Attendance   ☐
                                   Secretary?

PRODUCTIVITY PROBLEMS

Have you tried -   talking with the student?   ☐

                                   making arrangements with the student   ☐
                                   for extra help?

                                   referring the student to People Place   ☐

                                   reassessing the student's ability to   ☐
                                   cope with the course level of difficulty?

                                   consulting with parents?   ☐

APPLICATION PROBLEMS

Have you tried -   talking with the student?   ☐

                                   consulting with People Place?   ☐

                                   routing the student through normal   ☐
                                   disciplinary procedures?

                                   consulting with parents?   ☐

LIST OTHER RECOURSES YOU HAVE TRIED.

REASON FOR REFERRAL (Attendance, Productivity, Application)

Committee Use

RETURN COMPLETED FORM TO RECEPTIONIST

NDSS

■ **FIRE form**

jeopardy for the school's chronic student offenders had been saved. According to Dollack, (HIRE)FIRE was "a bottom line" that set the kinds of limits that people need.[11]

FIRE can be read differently. As discourse, it constructs learning within a paradigm of "really useful knowledge" in which students are trained less to think than they are structured into the need, coercively enforced, to obey and produce. Inasmuch as the explicit language of FIRE signifies the power of capital *over* labour, the "limits" and "bottom lines" that

---

```
                           S A M P L E

                    CONTRACT FOR:  ...........

DURATION:  November 18 to December 18, 1987.

PROBLEM AREAS:  Attendance in Homeroom, Per 1, 2, 3.
                Punctuality - frequently late.
                Productivity - low.
                Application - poor.
                Behaviour - inappropriate.

TERMS:
     1.  Will attend all classes including Homeroom.
     2.  Will be on time for classes.
     3.  Will be allowed from November 18 to December 4 to get caught up
         on missing assignments.
         By December 4 all 3 of    teachers must indicate that missing
         assignments are caught up.
     4.  On December 18 all work must be up to date and attendance must
         be perfect.
     5.  Behaviour and Language -    must refrain from using improper
         language (swearing) and must behave in an appropriate manner.

NOTES:
     1.  If     is ill the school is to be notified by the parents.
     2.  If     becomes ill during the day and has to leave school, he must
         get approval through the attendance office - BEFORE LEAVING.
         The attendance office will notify the parents.
     3.  If     is removed from class for rude language or behaviour the
         contract will be regarded as being broken.

CONSEQUENCES:

     Failure to comply with the conditions of the contract will result
     in the loss of all possible credits.    will then be required to
     complete the career search program on an independent basis. If this
     happens the parents will be notified immediately.    may be able to
     return to a regular program for Semester 2.

SIGNATURES:
     For School:
     Parents:
     Student:
```

NDSS

■ **FIRE contract**

NDSS administrators extol as necessary to "human nature" are nothing less than class boundaries established by state power masquerading as "education." Moreover, the issue is not so much the few students who, in the eyes of subject teachers and administrators, require the scrutiny of FIRE. As educational and cultural commentator Paul Willis notes, "If 'trouble makers' are locked away, some of the cultural and social processes which helped to form them will be locked away (not destroyed), too. And if individual and certain kinds of psychological categories reign supreme ... then general social processes can soon be turned into personal 'failings.'"[12]

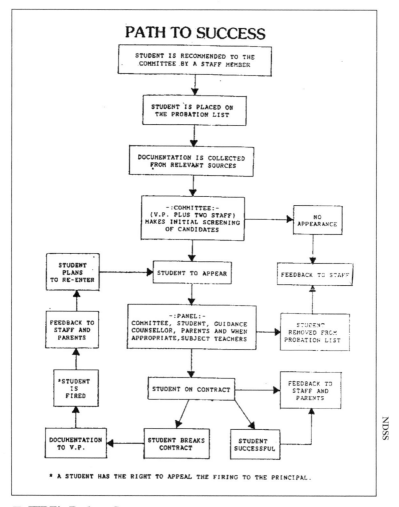

■ FIRE's Path to Success

The importance of a program such as FIRE, then, is not so much what it does for students with problems. Rather, its significance lies in how it constructs the ongoing, everyday oppositions of high-school life — student/teacher, good behaviour/bad behaviour, success/failure — on a terrain in which everything can be related to a conception of work stripped of discontent, alienation, and resistance and sustained only as duty and responsibility. Messages go out to delinquent and diligent alike. When coercive authority is invoked it isolates and detaches not only individuals but also the social experience of defiance and defeat. This is indeed an education.

"They tried to make us into a company," one NDSS graduate recalls.[13] Students at NDSS are truly, "learning a living," and that living is walled in by the constraints and powers of capital and property, which are usefully served by a training in which wage labour entails necessary attitudinal and practical responsibilities. Universalized as unchallengeable, common-sensical "givens," such appropriate behaviour is thus taught as human need, rather than being situated within relations of class struggle.

These lessons were reinforced through the increasingly materialized informal relationship of Goodyear and NDSS. The ties solidified before the plant opened, deepened as Goodyear recruited its original work-force in the late 1980s, and continued apace with the tire production of the 1990s. The company turned government corporate handouts into an initial "investment" donation of generic equipment, valued at $100,000. Over the course of the next few years, Principal Dollack estimates, Goodyear supplied the school with hundreds of thousands of dollars worth of supplies, ranging from industrial welders to paint brushes; the industrial physics program, and its head, Dick Hopkins, were especially favoured by Goodyear's gifts.

The federally funded Commercial Industrial Training Committee paid the salaries of four instructors and a secretary hired by NDSS to run a training program for Goodyear workers, and the federal Skills Development Branch of Manpower was further tapped in the effort to raise the almost $450,000 needed to sustain the project. Running from 2:30 in the afternoon to 11:30 at night, five days a week for three to four months, the training program began in January 1989 and, over the course of two phases, processed about three hundred Goodyear workers. Instructors were hired by Hughes, O'Connor, Board of Education superintendent Ed Thompson, and Goodyear personnel through the

Napanee offices of the Canada Employment Centre, but the teachers quickly became employees of Goodyear, not NDSS. Using a $130,000-$170,000 grant from Skills Quinte (a federally funded industrial training committee based in nearby Belleville), NDSS leased equipment needed in the training program, and technology specific to the Goodyear operation was supplied on (quasi-permanent) loan by the company.

Students began to express irritation at Goodyear's privileged place within NDSS, especially when they lost parking-lot spaces to company trainees. But this hardly made a dent in the administrative commitment of the school to the corporation. By March 1993 a third session was about to begin at NDSS, with the school's usual "fee-for-service" paid by Goodyear through resources and materials donated.[14]

Perhaps the most visible Goodyear-NDSS link was forged in the highly publicized role the high school played as a virtual hiring centre for the new company. After Goodyear announced in November 1988 that it would be looking for the first of its new workers, sixty maintenance-technician trainees, over one thousand applicants, some from as far away as Nova Scotia, descended on both the Canada Employment Centre and the NDSS. Knowing that the sheer number of applicants would strain the physical capacities of the local Employment Centre office and staff, NDSS opened its doors, serving Goodyear and the Canadian state as a surrogate employment and immigration centre. Rod Hughes announced that resumes were being accepted at NDSS, but that prospective Goodyear employees had to show up in person to be interviewed and get their application forms scrutinized. Most of the job seekers were between twenty and thirty years of age, with roughly one-half of them women. Five months later, on April Fool's Day 1989, the Canada Employment and Immigration office no longer even attempted to process applications, but instead shifted its quadrupled thirty-member staff to the NDSS gymnasium on a Saturday, where, along with ten police officers and six parking attendants paid by Goodyear, it handled 2,500 applications for four hundred production jobs. The applicants were an older lot, but their numbers never reached the five thousand expected. Some were lined up outside NDSS at 3:00 A.M. on Saturday morning, and when the doors opened at 5:30 there were 1,300 applicants waiting to get inside. Years later, with a mere 130 jobs at stake, 2,700 applicants showed up at NDSS, the numbers seeking work bloated by the plant closures and unemployment of a recessionary downturn. They came from as far away as Barrie and Kitchener, where tire plants had closed their doors in the late 1980s. According to the Napanee plant's communications officer, Shelley Aylesworth-Spink, "It was pretty crazy."[15]

After half a decade of activity, the Goodyear-NDSS connection is now unmistakable. There are no committees and formal institutional arrangements linking the company and the local high school, but everyone knows of the intimate, if informal, relationship. Most NDSS faculty have toured the plant — although other people in the area are denied similar access — and school staff meetings have been held at the Goodyear site. When the new plant wins awards, it takes the time to invite NDSS administrators to the celebrations and praises the quality of secondary education in Lennox and Addington County. Industrial physics teacher Dick Hopkins depends on Goodyear for resources and materials provided on a monthly basis.[16] But the Goodyear "gift" is not without its rewards. Students produce for the company: Goodyear engineer Andrew Walker and production support technician Brad Young consult with Hopkins and his pupils, describing specific plant needs and suggesting projects that could be worked on at NDSS. In 1992-93, for

■ **Goodyear employment application**

instance, Grade 12 students in industrial physics, in consultation with Walker, designed and built a polygum separator machine called "the Hawk." For $4,000 worth of materials Goodyear secured a mechanized way of reducing labour time and intensifying the work process, upping productivity considerably. Months later, the Napanee Goodyear plant's internal newsletter, *Tire Tracks*, declared a "partnership," noting that students in six different NDSS classes had "become part of Goodyear Napanee's business." They created a Spiral Overlay Transportation Unit, improving Goodyear's efficiency by eliminating problems inherent in an early system that tended to deform spools by shifting them within the plant on pins.

Praising the benefits accruing to the students with this direct research and development activity, and extolling the "teamwork" exhibited by Goodyear and NDSS, Walker likened these kinds of projects to "contracting out work from a company."[17] He was right: through its relationship to Goodyear, Napanee District Secondary School had indeed become something of a company — one in which the workers received only the wages of incorporation and the price of the product was paid in kind with the bestowal of "gifts."[18]

Chapter Six

Tithing Tire Production:
Or, the Goodyear Squeaky Wheel Gets State Oil

It is better to give than to receive, Goodyear's promoters would have us believe. The company makes much of its local charitable contributions, tallied at $50,000 in 1992. "Team members" raised $48,000 for the United Way, and although these "gifts" came from the workers and managerial staff, Goodyear itself supplies scoreboards for local ball diamonds and participates in regional parades, festivals, and tournaments, as well as contributing to the needs of vocational training at NDSS.[1] Yet the "gift" is not a one-way street. Whatever is given, one suspects, has its benefits in tax write-offs. But mere depreciation of capital expenditure and revenue write-offs were never enough for the Akron multinational. Goodyear got as good as it gave; indeed, it made sure early on that it was on the receiving end of state largesse.

The training program grants filtered through NDSS and the Lennox and Addington County Board of Education were obviously little more than subsidies sustaining Goodyear's initial labour recruitment costs. But they were a drop in the bucket compared to the megabucks Goodyear literally demanded from various wings of the Canadian state. As the anonymity and secrecy of Goodyear's invasion of Napanee broke in the winter of 1988, the company made it quite clear that until specific aid and duty/tax concessions were secured from the provincial and federal governments, there would be no official announcement of the Akron firm setting up a Napanee branch plant. With the number of paid positions associated with the plant inflated to eight hundred, Peter Rose, a Goodyear public relations spokesman, declared on 24 March 1988: "Until a final and satisfactory decision is made, there is no investment, no plant, and no jobs." A day later Goodyear Canada president Scott Buzby indicated that the entire undertaking hung on the thread of federal funding. "We're not in a position as yet to make a final decision on the project," he commented, indicating that the company's "partners in Ottawa" (the federal government) had not yet delivered the required economic goods. "We're confident it will happen," Buzby concluded. "But I have to wait until the cheque's in the mail."

To make sure that there was no political dragging of the subsidy feet, Lennox and Addington County councillors blanketed various levels of the state, from Prime Minister Brian Mulroney and Ontario Premier David Peterson through government ministries to adjoining regional councils, with communications urging that elected officials get involved with the program of corporate enticement. They wanted the governments of Canada and Ontario to "make every possible effort to ensure that Goodyear of Canada Ltd. may proceed with the establishment of a manufacturing facility." Member of Parliament Bill Vankoughnet wasted no time in declaring the town of Napanee "open for business"; his next act was to visit the Goodyear plant in Greece. A provincial counterpart, Keith MacDonald, called the Goodyear plant "the greatest thing that's happened to eastern Ontario in the past 55 years." Local provincial court judge Peter Coulson also endorsed Goodyear: "The best sentence I could give out to our kids would be a steady job. Too many of them get into trouble because they're out of work here."

Indeed, so exuberant were the politicians to grease the squeaky, economically demanding Goodyear wheel with state oil that they jumped the gun and leaked the news of the company's plans, forcing Akron officials to make their intentions public for the first time. "Some of our friends in Queen's Park were so excited they couldn't contain themselves," Buzby confessed.[2]

When the cheques, endorsed by the state and payable to Goodyear, were added up, the sums were not inconsiderable. Provided that the company completed construction of the plant in two phases, culminating in capacity-production by 1994, the Ontario government agreed to provide $32 million (or a full 10 per cent of the total plant investment) in the form of an interest-free loan, payable (in depreciated dollars) over ten years. Ottawa's federal government had already announced in January that it had earmarked $125 million for the remission of duties on goods imported by the major Canadian tire producers: Michelin, Goodyear, and Uniroyal-Goodrich. Goodyear's share of this rebate was estimated at $25 million.

According to Patrick Boyer, Progressive Conservative MP from the Etobicoke-Lakeshore riding where Goodyear's factory closed in 1987, the company exploited this remission duty program, abusing its original intentions. Ostensibly aimed at correcting "technical anomalies on customs duties and payments" and dealing with "minor inequities and injustices," the duty remission orders covered by the federal Financial Administration Act were now being used to fund plant shutdowns and relocations, providing massive corporate handouts without parliamentary approval.

There was talk of Goodyear also seeking assistance from Canada Employment and Immigration as well as the federal Department of Regional and Industrial Expansion, but the minister, Robert de Cotret, refused to discuss the matter, citing the possibility of a breach of confidentiality. As Ontario Opposition Leader Bob Rae, his NDP colleague Ruth Grier, and Boyer hammered away at the state's willingness to cater to Goodyear's demands, it was announced that Goodyear was to get a further $38 million in its duty subsidy. When questioned about this tax break, one Ministry of Finance figure justified it quickly and easily: "A $320-million investment and 800 jobs — that's why."

Meanwhile, Goodyear Canada made no bones about upping its levy to the Ohio parent to an annual $30 million, prompting an irate Boyer to conclude, "Goodyear Canada is merely a conduit for Canadian tax dollars going to Akron." When minority shareholders in Goodyear Canada got wind of the financial drain south, they launched a public attack, chastising Goodyear for depriving shareholders of their rightful dividends: "It's reprehensible, wrong, and robbery," one investor said. "If the company wanted to get the money out, they should pay a special dividend. Goodyear is acting as if it didn't have any minority shareholders." The NDP's Rae saw the situation as yet another case of multinationals "playing the governments off each other for funds." The tragedy, according to Rae, was that the Ontario taxpayer was being asked to foot the bill for factory closures. Boyer attacked the rule of his own Conservative Party, questioning the federal government's "political morality" and condemning its "failure to govern in the interests of the country and the people."[3]

Assailed from the right and the left, with disgruntled Bay Street investors and Tory and NDP politicians alike clamouring for inquiries and voicing their varied discontents, Goodyear was seemingly placed on the defensive. But it remained complacently aggressive in the face of this hostility. The company had every reason to ignore its critics. While they moaned, it was on its way to the bank. Silent in the face of stock-holder protests, the company easily weathered the storm of investor dis-content. From the Ministry of State for Small Business, Thomas Hockin declared that the levy to corporate headquarters in the United States did "not appear to be out of order in any way." The Ontario govern-ment's Resources Development Committee heard testimony on the Etobicoke plant closure, but it amounted to little more than letting steam get blown off rather than forcing it to be repressively and danger-ously contained. A state-sponsored employee assistance committee, established in the wake of the Etobicoke plant's 1987 shutdown, con-cluded, "The company acted responsibly."[4]

Thus, as political critics shouted the alarm and the workers got burnt, Goodyear fiddled and took time to count the more substantive material blessings provided by its friends in state office. The firm had in fact done well for itself: when Honda moved into Alliston, Ontario, it received nothing from the Canadian state. The com-pany also had no trouble raising $200 million from a group of six leading Canadian lending institu-tions, and in 1992 the fed-eral government quietly extended the duty remis-sions for Goodyear and other tire manufacturers a further five years.[5]

Corporate figureheads were understandably elat-ed. Goodyear Canada's Buzby sounded the corpo-ratist ideological note of "teamwork." He stressed: "All of this is really a joint effort. It's not just us at Goodyear. It's us, the folks

Whig-Standard

■ **Goodyear Canada President (1988), Scott Buzby**

in Napanee, and the provincial and federal governments. We can all take the credit and enjoy the benefits." Goodyear public relations officer Rose concluded that everyone was going to win with Goodyear coming to Napanee and that this was the beginning of a long-lasting "partnership and marriage."

Indeed, metaphors of holy matrimony dominated the rhetoric of the announcement of Goodyear coming to Napanee. "We'll be back soon to get us up to the altar and make it official," Buzby said.[6] But as it turned out, some good citizens were not to be invited to the wedding.

Whig-Standard

■ **Capital and the State: Napanee plant manager K. B. Kleckner and Liberal Premier of Ontario (1988), David Peterson.**

Chapter Seven

The Goodyear Family: Union without a UNION

A distinct part of the hue and cry about Goodyear's successes with state subsidies related to organized labour. Napanee's new Goodyear plant was erected on the ruins of the old factory on Lakeshore Drive in Etobicoke, just outside Toronto. That plant, described by one corporate manager as "a multi-storey building which shakes on its foundations," was a dinosaur-structure from the smokestack age. But it had employed 1,574 workers, most of them affiliated with Local 232 of the United Rubber, Cork, Linoleum and Plastics Workers of America, established in 1942.[1]

Goodyear's plant in Etobicoke (or New Toronto, as Etobicoke was historically and colloquially known) was central in the development of the area as one of Ontario's most industrialized sectors. At one time New Toronto was reputed to "have the highest value of manufacturing per square mile in North America." By the 1940s and 1950s the larger Etobicoke-Lakeshore region boasted a distinct working-class identity, separate from Toronto and proud of its established industrial base. The corporation's "cloak and dagger" property drive in eastern Ontario began at about the same time as the New Toronto plant closed its doors in 1987, throwing hundreds of workers onto the unemployment line, accelerating the process of coerced deindustrialization that saw Etobicoke-Lakeshore decimated by "downsizing," "relocation," and "closure" of its once continentally renowned factories.

J.R. Morris, a former businessman appointed chair of the Goodyear Employee Assistance Committee, reported that the plant shutdown engendered lasting feelings of betrayal and bitterness among the employees who had lost their jobs. "Newspaper reports of the new plant planned for Napanee, Ontario were irritating to a number of employees," he said. This was perhaps something of an understatement. When Napanee's Goodyear fanfare was burning brightly in 1988, the fires of resentment in Etobicoke were dying down, but the embers of trade union antagonism would glow well into the 1990s.[2]

State officials tried to douse this class heat with wet promises that any government aid to Goodyear would contain "labour provisions," but nothing close to this materialized. Bob Rae, Ontario opposition leader and later premier under the New Democratic Party (NDP), talked tough but carried a weak stick. Insisting that there should be no government aid unless workers laid off at Etobicoke got the option of being rehired, and that the province's ruling Liberals under Premier David Peterson must demand recognition of the United Rubber Workers (URW) as the acknowledged collective bargaining agent in the new plant, Rae pontificated: "It's outrageous that the government would be doing this without a guarantee that the workers who've given 20, 30 years of their lives to the Goodyear company wouldn't get a guarantee of a job at that new plant. It's clear that we still have a rule by a few multinational companies in this province [and] that they can still pretty well do what they like, and the workers ... don't have very many rights at all."

Similar sentiments were expressed by the Etobicoke-Lakeshore members of both the provincial and federal parliaments. They deplored the blatant transparency of a company seeking lucrative state favours when it was shutting down operations in one locale and reopening elsewhere. Ruth Grier, the local NDP member of the provincial legislature, went on the attack: "These corporations are like cannibals. They eat the workers up and then spit them out. They dump all the injuries and all the family problems on the community." Local 232 president David Birrell called for the Ontario government to demand a priority hiring pledge from Goodyear ensuring that sacked workers would be first in line for any employment possibilities in the years to come. Even the Conservative Party's Patrick Boyer was able to see that the state was bankrolling union busting. He argued that the hidden agenda of Goodyear's relocation was a purposeful effort to rid itself of the irksome presence of organized labour. The veil of secrecy draped over the provincial-company negotiations around financial aid only worsened the situation, as did Goodyear's record at the Etobicoke plant. Indeed the closing of the Etobicoke plant, as Goodyear Employee Assistance Committee chair Morris would later note, provided cause to explore the problematic meanings and contradictions of "the Goodyear ideology."[3]

The Etobicoke/New Toronto plant was, according to Goodyear's own publication, *The Wingfoot Clan*, "the flagship of Canadian operations for the 70 years of its life." Built in 1917 on a twenty-three-acre site, attracted by the civic carrot of access to unlimited water supplies, and hailed (as would later be Napanee) as "the most modern rubber factory in the world," the plant signalled the arrival of modern industry in the New Toronto area. The multistorey factory, distinguished by its huge smokestack, had its floor spacing expanded more than five times, eventually reaching 1.4 million square feet. It employed 1,500 workers by 1922, and at its peak in the 1980s it provided jobs for more than 1,900 (union officials suggested an even larger workforce of over 2,500 in the 1960s). The Goodyear factory was so huge that women who worked there in the 1940s and 1950s recall taking their roller skates to work and skating during breaks and before and after their shifts.

From an original capacity of 200 tires daily, plant output soared to 10,500 during World War II and may have climbed to as high as 17,000 by the eve of the plant closure. Long denigrated as obsolete, the Etobicoke factory nevertheless saw significant infusions of capital in various modernization ventures, most notably a sustained $32-million improvement effort throughout the early to mid-1980s. Redesigning production flow, importing new equipment, implementing a work schedule of six and two-thirds days with four production shifts, and mobilizing sales, the management of Goodyear Canada gave the impression that it was intending to build tires in the Toronto area for at least a few years more.

The New Toronto facility was a model of Litchfieldian productive paternalism. Besides its own Flying Squadron it had a Top Ten Club composed of supervisors whose proven company loyalty exhibited itself in meeting corporate objectives and integrating themselves into the senior citizen events, charity drives, and youth sports central to the community-Goodyear connection long cherished by Akron's tire bosses. A vibrant recreational club orchestrated leisure activities for workers. There were company ball diamonds, bowling alleys on the second floor of the factory, industrial sport leagues, a rifle range, and annual summer picnics and Christmas parties for children. Fading with the advent of television, and possibly challenged by the United Rubber Workers' forays into the cultural field, these company-sponsored leisure programs were seen as part of the success of the Goodyear "family" in consolidating production and quieting worker discontent.

Proud and self-promotional, the company proclaimed itself "a good neighbour" and "a leader in the industrial family of New Toronto." The "Goodyear ideology" of labour-management co-operation was promoted by tire company officials to the bitter end. Canadian president Scott Buzby proclaimed: "I want to emphasize that the plant closure in no way reflects the quality of support of Toronto plant employees. Unionized and salaried employees have responded well to our productivity programs." Yet even *The Wingfoot Clan*, in constructing the Litchfieldian mythology of class harmony, familialist unity, and corporate-community bonds, could not help but stumble over the awkward tensions of the 1987 plant shutdown that threw almost 1,600 Goodyear "sons and daughters" on the unemployment lines:

> When the plant closed its doors for the last time, more than a manufacturing facility was gone. Over the years, the plant and its employees had established a presence in the community that transcended commercial considerations. They were the heart of a vital industrial area. It is unfortunate that, after such an eventful and productive history, the plant closed amidst controversy. Hopefully, it will be remembered more for its fruitful life and positive contributions than for its passing.

Ever hopeful where its image was concerned, Goodyear's task in 1987 was one of damage control. The challenge would come largely from its disgruntled unionized workers.[4]

Non-union for the first seventeen years of its history, the Etobicoke factory staved off the threat of labour organization in the 1930s and early 1940s with a company-sponsored representational plan known as the "Joint Conference." This company union collapsed in 1942, after the Goodyear plant in Bowmanville, Ontario, organized with the Rubber Workers and the New Toronto employees rebelled against the company's arbitrary firing of a worker in an attempt to implement production speed-up. Propaganda sheets such as the "Bulletin" and the "Slingfoot Gang" talked up the prospects of the new CIO union, and when the company-resisted certification vote occurred late in 1942 the United Rubber Workers were recognized as the official bargaining agent of the Goodyear employees. Throughout the 1940s and 1950s Local 232 of the United Rubber, Cork, Linoleum and Plastics Workers of America was a visible, public presence in the Toronto labour movement, especially on Labour Day, when the union often won prizes for the most members on parade or the best float.

Strikes and lockouts were rare occurrences in the history of the local, but Goodyear workers joined masses of other Canadian unionists in a post-World War II upheaval. They sustained a four-month strike in 1946, walked off the job for eighteen days in 1951, and fought a lengthy battle in 1974. Supported by an impressive women's auxiliary, proud owner of a Union Hall that served as a centre of sociability as well as labour meetings, and publisher for many years of its own newspaper, *New Advocate*, Local 232 was a brake on Goodyear's effort to roll back any semblance of worker autonomy and self-activity.[5]

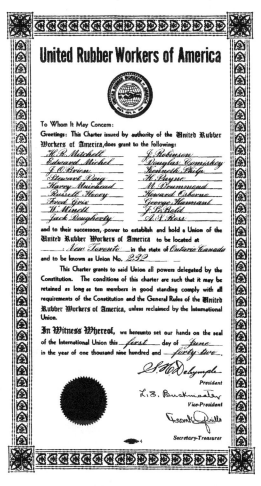

Local 232/Etobicoke

■ **Local 232 Charter**

As the company and the union locked horns in countless negotiating battles, a common corporate refrain was that the plant would eventually have to be closed given its outmoded four-storey architecture and structural instability. Union leaders came to regard these combative proclamations, uttered time and time again over the course of decades, as threatening bluffs. Lulled into a kind of disbelief concerning the possibility of plant shutdown, workers at Etobicoke's Goodyear operation thought the company's massive restructuring of the plant in the mid-1980s, which included a huge movement of machinery to a former administrative division on the fourth floor, indicated a commitment to continuity of production and jobs. Conceding "cross crafting," a loosening of union work rules, and agreeing to a switch-over to twelve-hour shifts, Local 232 saw itself as doing its part to work with management to bring costs down and raise plant productivity.

Workers were dubious about the move to the fourth floor. They were skeptical about the structure's capacity to sustain the immense weight of radial tire machinery. But they did their best to make things work. The union participated in the introduction of the "team concept" in the aftermath of a 1983 contract settlement. When Akron appointed new plant supervisory personnel, notably plant manager Mike Sterling, workplace relations took a detour off the class road of "hard knocks." Indeed, to union leader Birrell, the new managerial style of the 1980s, with its emphasis on downplaying supervisory coercion and a new reliance on worker self-motivation, was "almost like a breath of fresh air." Things appeared to be going well. But Birrell also sensed that the shifting contours of class relations in the 1980s were more apparent than real. They "don't fight you with a baseball bat" any more, he now says. "They do you in with a briefcase."[6]

The opening shot in the briefcase wars that would end with the demise of Goodyear's Etobicoke operation was in fact a highly successful corporate diversion. In November 1986 Goodyear faced a hostile takeover by the colourful, mythologically larger-than-life Sir James Goldsmith. Aligned with the brokerage firm Merrill Lynch, Goldsmith, an Anglo-French Rothschild-family-connected corporate raider, would come to be known in the locker-room atmosphere of Akron head office as "Goldenballs." He had an infamous reputation for buying up companies, gutting them, and walking away with a tidy fortune. Claiming that Goodyear had embarked on an irresponsible diversification binge, diluting its managerial expertise in unprofitable and unwise acquisitions that ill served its shareholders, Goldsmith launched one of his trademark "commando style raids" on the Ohio tiremaker. Managing to acquire 12.5 million shares of Goodyear Tire and Rubber stock, he almost pulled it off.[7]

What he had not counted on was Goodyear's material commitment to its own familialist ideology. The company wanted no part of a Goldsmith takeover; it could not fathom losing control to an outsider. To the staid middle-American "down-homers" at the helm of Goodyear Tire and Rubber, Sir James was certainly an outsider, easily constructed as the dangerous unknown "other." Renowned for his tenacious refusal to be bought out of his takeover bids by "greenmail," Goldsmith had obviously never come up against the likes of Litchfield's heirs in Akron. Goodyear promptly whipped its "family" into line, calling on members of the wingfoot clan in places high and low. Representative John Seiberling, an Ohio Democrat whose forefathers had founded Goodyear, was quickly brought on side. He arranged a House of Congress subcommittee hearing on the takeover bid and contacted United Rubber Workers union officials in an effort to solidify their opposition to Goldsmith.

If some union leaders, including Local 232's newly elected president David Birrell, were skeptical of championing their employer over Goldsmith, others were far from shy about crossing class lines: Local 2 of the URW "approved a resolution urging members to give up four weeks of pay to buy the stock." One worker sounded a dissident note of class consciousness, pointing out that no one on the anti-Goldsmith bandwagon was calling for the end of government subsidies to plant relocations overseas, where unions were non-existent and wages and conditions inferior to those in the United States. In all the fuss about Goldsmith, he pointed out, there was no mention of worker protection such as plant closing legislation. "Goodyear has no allegiance to its workforce, to Akron, or to the nation," he argued. "Like all multinationals, its allegiance is to the almighty dollar. Working people should be fighting our own battles and advancing our own agenda. Let the sharks have at each other."

Yet this was not the dominant theme of class relations in the Goldsmith-charged atmosphere of November 1986. Officials from thirty-six union locals across the United States and Canada were summoned to Akron, where they met with Goodyear executives. Needing working-class support, Goodyear courted the bureaucratic representatives of their class adversaries. To sweeten the pot for the rubberworkers' union, Goodyear was said to be considering implementing a successor clause in the international's master agreement with the company — an addition that would bind any purchaser of Goodyear property to the terms and conditions of the contract with the union. Previously reluctant to grant such a concession because it lessened the market possibilities for sale of individual Goodyear plants and subsidiaries, Akron was now reconsidering the matter in the face of the Goldsmith challenge.

Signs of protest dotted lawns in Akron. Hundreds of people, including the pupils in a Grade Four class, wrote to express their revulsion at the Goldsmith takeover.

When Goldsmith appeared before the Congress subcommittee he protested being scapegoated for his "foreign" origin. He said he thought the United States welcomed foreign investment, pointing out as well that Goodyear was active in twenty-seven countries. Meanwhile Ohio anti-takeover legislation was being "drafted and proposed for immediate passage." "Who the hell are you!" thundered John Seiberling in a macho explosion of resentment against an "outsider."[8]

As the counter-Goldsmith campaign escalated, the rhetoric of Goodyear spokesmen dipped into the deep ideological reservoir of familialist producerism and industrial republicanism. Themes of family and nation were never far from the surface of protest. Disgruntled that government required antitrust reviews of corporate mergers — a union of "consenting adults"— but saw no need to investigate "foreign" takeovers, Goodyear chairman and chief executive officer Robert E. Mercer concluded, "The law regulates marriages, but totally ignores rape, which is what I call it." Before Congress Mercer pleaded for the cause of Americanism and productivity: "While there is still time for our nation, I urge you to put some reasonable curbs on the activity that is sapping more and more of America's industrial strength." Goodyear Canada head Buzby simply put himself on the record as opposed to "cowboy capitalism," taking his stand against those "quick-buck artists" like Goldsmith who would take "the cash and run." Such people "feel no responsibility for communities and employees." This would, in the months to come, sound a bit like the pot calling the kettle black, especially on Lakeshore Drive in Etobicoke.[9]

The temerity of Goldsmith, who threatened to outflank Goodyear with the sheer weight of a crude cash putsch, obviously registered with Akron's tire overlords. They took the buyout bid seriously. Mobilizing their resources they fought back politically and economically. It proved too much for Goldsmith, who recognized the political opposition as overwhelming and engaged in some classic profit-taking. The mythic Goldenballs, reputed to be the investment community's biggest gambler, a man who "hates to feel safe" and stops only when "the deals — the game — cease to amuse him," apparently chose to accept the lucrative "greenmail" Akron scraped up and lost his acquisitive sense of humour. Goodyear bought all of Goldsmith's shares, accounting for 11.5 per cent of the company's stock, and to try to ensure that they never faced another Wall Street raid they put offers out on forty million other shares. At $50 per share the cost was truly astounding, reaching $2.6 billion. Goldsmith himself walked away with $620 million and $37 million in expenses. When the fur stopped flying from this "financial cat fight" Goodyear was saddled with a ballooning debt, reputed to be in the $3-4 billion range by the early 1990s. Servicing the debt alone cost Goodyear $1 million daily in the late 1980s, and the firm sold off assets such as the oil and gas Celeron Corporation of Texas, the 22,000-acre Arizona resort and farm properties acquired under Litchfield in 1916, and some of its small Canadian manufacturing concerns. It cut back its global workforce from the 134,000 on the payroll in 1985 to 116,000 in 1987; further labour reductions brought the number of Goodyear workers down to 105,000 by 1991. Even Robert G. Mercer, son of the boss, eventually got the axe. The Washington public relations figure took it stoically: "I have to realize Goodyear is not part of the family any more." As the Goodyear vs. Goldsmith post-mortem was filed, each side taking credit for the supposed new financial health of the Akron multinational, other corporate raiders were rumoured to be contemplating another takeover bid.[10]

On November 20, 1986, all Goodyear employees, including those at the New Toronto tire plant, received a warm "Dear Employee" letter from Robert E. Mercer. It commenced with thanks to all of the workers, union leaders, legislators, community officials, and others who had supported Goodyear against Goldsmith. Corporate familialism and Americanism were blurred yet again: "All can take great pride in demonstrating that we and other Americans value the industries built up over many years with hard work and dedication, and won't stand idly by when they are threatened. In my opinion, the sight of whole communities rising up against an unwarranted takeover attempt was the major factor in Goldsmith's decision to sell out." Mercer extolled "the Goodyear name" as something "still ours to maintain, cherish, and protect," adding that all Goodyear employees had "exhibited the Goodyear spirit that truly does set us apart." He concluded that not only had "the Goodyear family" shown Goldsmith and others what they were all about, but it had also reminded "our nation that staying competitive in world trade requires something more than leaving American industry vulnerable to sneak attacks on the stock market."

It was vintage familialist Litchfieldian industrial republicanism. For members of Local 232, it was a colonial extension. But the national question hardly mattered in late November in Etobicoke: the Goodyear workers sighed in relief; they thought their jobs were now secure.

One day later, on November 21, 1986, Scott Buzby informed the employees at the Etobicoke facility that restructuring necessitated by the debt load incurred in thwarting Goldsmith's takeover was forcing the closing of the factory. The situation would, he said, result in "a major and permanent layoff of the plant's salaried and unionized employees." At the Friday afternoon shift-change, workers got wind of their dismal economic future.

"I got the good news," one truck driver with twenty-eight years of Goodyear service said. "It hurt — like a punch in the mouth." Leo Pardy, Local 232 treasurer-elect, couldn't "believe it." He said, "We were on top of the world because we thought we'd won the takeover battle. Then the company turns around and says we've got no jobs. It was down and dirty." What a difference a day made.[11]

Buzby later claimed that any hope of saving the sixteen-hundred Goodyear jobs in Etobicoke disappeared with Goldsmith. It was a position adopted in the months to come by virtually every company official: "The luxury of a long-term outlook was no longer possible. The raider had a notorious track record of hostile takeover and subsequent dismemberment and dissolution of companies. We fought for our life." According to Buzby, the restructuring of the corporation, including the closing of "non-competitive plants," was "only one of the unpleasant decisions we were forced to make." He also insisted that the decision to close the New Toronto factory was made by Goodyear Canada, not the parent company. Apparently Akron had only emphasized the need to restructure.

But as one anonymous "Goodyear insider" suggests, the excuse of Goldsmith's takeover bid was a public rationalization for a corporate decision already made. The notion of the Canadian division operating autonomously was a fiction. Goodyear had been stripping its Canadian subsidiary of decision-making powers and centralizing them in Akron. In closing the Lakeshore facility, head office chopped an annual wage bill of $38 million, slashed the Canadian workforce by 25 per cent, prepared the way for a modernized new facility, and seriously eroded union strength in the central Canadian tire industry. Not known to act precipitously, the men from Akron hardly needed the economics of a Goldsmith to close down the seventy-year-old Etobicoke plant. They were going to do that anyway; Goldsmith provided them with a convenient rationale. The workers could now be painted as merely "victims of a takeover attempt," something entirely outside the responsibility of the Goodyear family. This, much of the workforce realized, was a classic case of "smoke and mirrors."[12]

Carol Condé & Karl Beveridge in collaboration with the C.E.W.C

THE BOTTOM LINE

■ **The Bottom Line: Plant closures, discarded union jacket, and the solitude of job loss.**

That the real issues in the 1987 plant shutdown in New Toronto centred on Akron's need for uninhibited control over all of its operations was borne out over the course of the 1987-92 years as the Ohio-based company clashed repeatedly with its Canadian minority shareholders, whom it wanted to buy out at share prices many of them felt were inadequate. As investors chafed under Akron's peremptory appropriation of Goodyear Canada's financial health, Buzby first tried to deflect shareholder opposition to "corporate colonialists ... the men from Akron" with suggestions that more shares might be offered to Canadians. But in the years to come this possibility failed to materialize. Instead, Akron cried economic wolf in the aftermath of Goldsmith. It devalued its Canadian stock and offered minority investors $48 a share, when some financial counsellors were suggesting a real value of upwards of $80-$120. Disgruntled players in Goodyear stock claimed that Akron had withdrawn $53.65 a share annually from the Canadian subsidiary, driving down the trading price. With United States analysts rating the North American tire industry as the best investment among ninety business sectors, and the new Goodyear Canada Napanee operation universally hailed as a flagship "state-of-the-art" facility poised to service 75 per cent of all future North American automobile growth, Canadian shareholders told Goodyear to take a financial hike. Only 10,000 of 288,000 shares, in the end, went to Goodyear at $48 in June 1992.

Somebody knew something. Less than a year later Goodyear Canada traded on the Toronto stock exchange at $64. Why the charades, when minority shareholders controlled less than 12 per cent of Goodyear Canada? The men from Akron, again, had deep pockets and thin skins. Nothing less than total control seemed acceptable to them. Business comment explained the Goodyear stock wars of the late 1980s and early 1990s as nothing less than a corporate penchant for a restructured amalgamation of its North American operations, a process the U.S. parent company wanted to implement without impediments of any kind. "Increased flexibility" was now the Akron watchword. "A bunch of pesky Canadian shareholders" were the last thing the Ohio tire bosses wanted to contend with.[13]

Well, perhaps not *the* last thing. Trade unionism was undoubtedly a peskier force than a scattered group of investors who could only make their discontents heard at annual meetings and lacked any power anyway. However subdued the URW was as a class opposition — and the trade union bureaucracy's decision to rally around Goodyear against Goldsmith exposed a fatal flaw in the perspective of the labour bosses — its very presence in the company's tire plants was resented. Faced with the news of the plant closure, Birrell commented: "It's pretty clear they want to be rid of the employees and the union."[14] The union, to be sure, was mostly gone: but the employees had certain economic rights that the URW was determined to try to safeguard. When the Etobicoke plant shut down Goodyear faced a series of challenges, displays of working-class anger and bitterness, and organized demonstrations (seven hundred to eight hundred strong). There were demands and complaints that registered loosely with politicians, cost Akron materially, and exposed Goodyear's pretence of familialist care for its workers as a purposeful sham — a posture aimed at keeping production levels high and public relations good.

On the shop floor, between the announcement of the Etobicoke factory's death in November 1986 and the actual nailing down of its coffin lid in May 1987 there was "seething resentment over the remote financial shenanigans." As Goodyear workers cleaned, packed up, and crated the fourth-floor tire-building machinery, they registered their hostility and resentment in vulgar graffiti scrawled on the equipment and its shipping containers. Directed at Goldsmith and those future workers who would use the displaced technology, these messages were a profoundly frustrated discourse of discontent. But the company threatened to close the plant early if workers disrupted production, and Buzby's November 21, 1986, letter ended on a note of commitment, not to the tire-building workforce, but to "the best in quality, value and service for our customers."

This was yet a further slap in the face to a largely middle-aged industrial workforce proud of its skills and output. "We didn't get that money handed to us," one bitter nineteen-year Goodyear veteran says. "It was on incentive. We *produced.*" Tire production indeed continued apace, with the union convinced that it was necessary to "prove" to Goodyear that the old Lakeshore factory and its aged workforce could be profitable. Birrell remembers the last days: "They were turning out a thousand tires on a twelve-hour shift, breaking all kinds of production records. It was as if they said, 'We'll show the bastards.'"[15]

Within a week of Buzby's declaration that the New Toronto plant was being closed, there was a flurry of meetings. Etobicoke Mayor

Bruce Sinclair publicly protested what he called a "body blow to the community," suggesting, "We should have all the flags at half mast." A political scramble to displace resentment began, and certain agents of the state seemed to go into an overdrive of denial, working to deflect the personal traumas of working-class victims with empty suggestions of hope. Goodyear preferred the hardened patriarchal path.

Buzby suggested that this act of economically necessary discipline hurt the company as much as it did the workers. "We at Goodyear don't like to see this happening," he said. "Our employees are like our family. But the company has been through an extremely severe situation and can't afford to maintain a high-cost, non-profitable plant."

Goodyear rebuffed offers of government aid and investment, making it abundantly clear that nothing would reverse its decision. A plea from the Ontario Minister of Industry, Hugh O'Neil, to see the company books and make a determination of plant profitability was curtly ignored, dismissed as an inappropriate incursion on managerial prerogatives. Rudely rebuked, provincial officials nevertheless met with Goodyear twice in late November. But the best they could come up with were exploratory proposals of a government-worker buyout of the plant, and talk of enticing another tire company to Ontario. Finally, in the face of an NDP demand that the ruling Liberals convene a review of the plant closing, there was a brief hearing that proved little more than a forum for Goodyear Canada to absolve itself of responsibility for dismantling Ontario's largest tire production facility.

Susan Meurer

■ **The Etobicoke Goodyear Smokestack: the levelling of a landmark by 14 pounds of dynamite, as seen from the roof of the United Rubber Workers' Hall, January 13, 1990.**

Throughout it all, Goodyear reiterated that the New Toronto building was of "no use to anyone" and complained loudly that its Goldsmith-induced financial constraints had impaled the company on the interest horns of its creditor consortium, which stipulated that 80 per cent of all proceeds from assets had to be turned towards servicing the multibillion-dollar debt principal. No new plant could be built by Goodyear under these circumstances, at least certainly not before 1990. "You have to remember that our friendly bankers have put very strong controls over our use of capital," explained Buzby. Goldsmith and the bankers were to blame, said the men from Akron; Goodyear, too, was a victim.[16]

You would have had a difficult time convincing the Goodyear tire builders, drivers, machinists, mail-room clerks, tuber operators, and other employees that the company hurt as much as they did. Workers with decades of Goodyear employment behind them had paid a price for their regular paycheques. They bore the physical scars of waged employment: back ailments, impaired hearing, mangled fingers, and loss of limbs.

Leaving a shift, covered with dust and fine rubber particles, Goodyear employees would head home, shower, and collapse into bed, only to wake up with their body imprint blackened on the linen. Their dreams and nightmares centred on building tires. For years after, some workers could not pass by the Lakeshore Drive plant without catching themselves in mid-stride, just about to try to enter the locked doors. Men with over twenty-eight years at the Goodyear plant asked rhetorically, "Who is going to hire a guy with Grade 11 in the shape I'm in?" One of them was Cory Maracle, forty-eight years old, who had been preceded in the plant by his father, who worked at Goodyear for twenty-five years. Suffering from a bad back, two bum knees, and arthritis in his "sausage-finger hands," Maracle was "the horse with the broken leg." His co-worker Leo Pardy had ruptured a disc in his back slinging tires in 1983.

The costs of the plant closure, then, registered in ways that went well beyond the economic, although there was an abundance of financial misery too. Workers who had grown used to economic security found themselves facing mortgages and car payments they could no longer afford. But the cruel blow to self-esteem was perhaps the most devastating. A counsellor who worked with the laid-off tire operatives through the Goodyear Employee Assistance Program (sponsored by the original Assistance Committee), talking to them at Humber College (Toronto) and the Union Hall, captured the tragic human consequences of lost employment:

> Their work defined them. They thought, "I'm a *rubber worker*, I'm a *Goodyear* worker." And they didn't just lose a job—though you should never underestimate the awfulness of that—but lots of them worked in teams, teams of two and four, and they lost their best buddy, too. The amazing thing is, these men have such incredible skills—not just what they did technically, but trouble-shooting, carpentry, fixing this and that, all the things they did in their lives. And now they're getting the impression from the world around them that they're worth nothing.

Konstanty Salewski was employed at Goodyear for over two decades. Afterwards, still unemployed after six months of job searching, he reported: "I eat and sleep irregularly. Everything is out of whack." Just one year shy of a full pension from Goodyear when he lost his job, Gerard St. Laurent countered the boosterism of the economic optimists. "There's not an economic boom. It's all an illusion," he told a reporter. "Mulroney gets up there and says they've created 900,000 jobs — yeah, $6 jobs.... The economic part of it is only for the business people. They're the ones who are making a fortune. The ideology is all wrong. You make profits for people for years and then they throw you out the door. You're just a number."[17]

The Goodyear Employee Assistance Committee, funded by the federal and provincial governments as well as the company, and staffed by Goodyear and United Rubber Worker officials, operated for almost two years at a cost of roughly $130,000. It found that most of its task centred on older workers whose command of the English language was weak. But if the committee eased some workers back into the labour pool and reduced anxieties and the loss of self-worth through its seminars and counselling, the plant closure nevertheless took a dramatic human toll. Roughly 700 Goodyear workers availed themselves of the various services of the Assistance Committee; 135 came up empty in the search for work; of those who found jobs, many took pay cuts and accepted employment that they found far from satisfying. "Of course I'll do anything," reported one Goodyear employee who, after nineteen years as a tuber operator, now cleaned offices with his wife four hours every night. "But I don't think I can go any lower."[18]

Through the tireless efforts of Susan Meurer, the Goodyear plant closure and its human costs left a record in the folk art of Canada's particular experience of deindustrialization. Meurer, who counselled the displaced Goodyear workers as part of the Employee Assistance Program, soon grasped that with the Etobicoke factory's shutdown the "cultural history" and workplace "folklore" of the rubber works was beginning to disappear. She saw how much the intense pain of forced unemployment had also become a casualty in the depersonalizing drift of media attention to the statistics of "economic restructuring."

With blunt effectiveness, Meurer's poem "Closure" addresses the "bottom line" of exploitation looked at from the vantage point of workers rather than profit-takers, dividend mongers, and accountants:

The business report in the
Globe and Mail hardly
takes up two inches of newsworthiness.
Goodyear Canada Inc.
"Profit for six months ended June
30, 1987, $12.4 million compared
with $7.3 million a year earlier."
But I know who earned every dollar
to make the two inches possible.

I've heard the days that make up
a $5 million working lifetime at a tire plant.
I spent a week with Mike, Alan, Leo, Gary, Fitzroy ...

On May 1 they became statistics
in a plant closure ledger.
Not even an ink stain in the company books.
Tire builder, compounder, mold man, bead man:
they created the $5 million.

What am I to think
of a company that reports record profits
when 1200 workers are terminated.
Some severance, early retirement,
six months of benefits, do these equal
a working life?

So I consider: what is $5 million
divided by 1200?
"Share profit $4.80 compared with
$2.81."
I see that the creators of the wealth
lose their jobs to ensure $2 profit increase
for those who never:
moved 40,000 tires a year;
built 250 radials a shift;
mixed tonnes of tire compound;
worked one hour in a tire plant.

When she penned these lines of verse, Meurer was also hard at work on a play, *The Shadowboxers*. Dramatizing the general plight of workers who lost their jobs through workplace shutdowns, Meurer's play eventually received an Ontario Arts Council grant offsetting the costs of production and performance. With the aid of musicians, professional actors, and directors, and the financial assistance and support of United Rubber Workers Local 232, *The Shadowboxers* was eventually staged in the old union hall of the laid-off Goodyear workers; it was later aired on CBC-Radio's *Morningside* program. A musical celebrating "the culture of work," the play features eight original songs written by Allen Booth, including a rousing picket-line medley, a love ballad, and other lyrical accounts of work and its discontents, including a Tom Waits-like number. Addressing the history of class relations, working conditions, labour's attempts to control the pace of work, the shock of plant closure, and the public and private traumas of adjusting to unemployment, *The Shadowboxers* is an aptly named theatrical depiction of the price workers pay when they are forced to fight an enemy they cannot touch. The jobs that have disappeared are, for all of the alienation and danger that defines their existence, even more oppressive when they fade into the realm of absence and recollection.

Former Goodyear workers built the props and sets, and unionists who wanted to participate had small parts written for them. Indeed, the six professional actors and actresses talked to the laid-off tire builders, and rehearsals were held in the union hall where workers watched the production evolve, commenting on its development. Parts of the play were staged to include the working-class audience as participants in pre-

■ *Shadowboxers* playwright, Susan Meurer,
and Local 232 officers with play props.

sentations of union meetings or protest demonstrations. Art and life
blurred as unionized actors represented workers who, as an audience,
then joined in the theatrical presentation of their own labour-related
experiences. All three live March 1989 performances were "packed and
well received." Meurer says, "At times the audience seemed totally
caught up in the action, shouting encouragement at the union meeting,
chanting at the demo, or voting on union decisions."

The Shadowboxers was an exhilarating and successful project precisely
because it was not foreign to the Goodyear workers, but a sensitive

Photos: David Smiley

■ *Shadowboxers*, Scene 1: On strike

■ Scene 2: Fighting back

■ **Scene 3: Addressing the workers**

■ **Scene 4: The domestic costs of plant closure**

■ **Scene 5: Want ads?**

reproduction of their labouring and domestic lives. Art worked, and work became art, scripted, staged, and sustained with actual working-class participation, as a kind of class struggle.[19]

Workers struggling in this way understandably reacted with considerable venom to the news that a new plant was to be built in Napanee. After claiming that it was cash-starved and could build no such plant — and maintaining this position throughout 1986 and into the early months of 1987 — Goodyear began to relax its purse strings and its hard-line posture in February 1987. By that time, most of the workers had cut their ties to Goodyear, so convinced were they that future employment was simply not in the cards. When Goodyear officially committed itself to building in Napanee in March 1988, the resentment and anger among its ex-workforce boiled over. David Birrell deplored the trickery of the company, which, he was convinced, denied its plans to build knowing that this would mislead workers into accepting benefits that would then disqualify them for any new tire-building employment. "Thoroughly pissed off," Birrell and others admitted that the news was "great for Napanee." But they asked, what about "guys that gave the best years of their lives? Should they just be thrown on the scrap heap?" One maintenance worker exploded: "They don't care about people who served the company for years. A lot of people were tricked by them."

The Goodyear ideology of the caring family hadn't just worn thin; it was blasted apart by workers who had long forgotten the company picnics, sporting teams, and Christmas parties of their past employment. They looked at the jubilant headlines about the Napanee plant, read of government handouts to their former boss, and snorted with defiant contempt, "Those are *our* jobs."[20]

For many former workers the final straw turned on the company's handling of severance and pension benefits. Goodyear advocates made much of the severance and pension settlement at Etobicoke, championing the company as a "good corporate citizen." Napanee Goodyear boosters hailed the payouts as ostensibly above the government guidelines, pegged at $66 million, with an average of $9,500 per employee — figures that seemed astronomical and generous in small-town Ontario. But these kind of numbers can be deceiving. They masked the inequitable manoeuvring that Goodyear's unionists challenged and partially turned aside in the years following the plant closure. Mythical averages and large pool sums mean far less, after all, to a huge, differentiated labour force, whose work time in the plant totalled tens of thousand of *years*. They provide no insight, moreover, into the intense animosity generated by company efforts to reduce the price of the shutdown's benefit bill, in the process rubbing union noses in the dirt of economic insult.

Goodyear began by offering its non-union salaried employees much better severance and pension terms. It appeared to want to punish organized labour, claiming that Goodyear's salaried employees could take advantage of a certain leeway associated with voluntary retirements and other options, but production workers would have to make do with the rigidities of collective agreements and the law. One irate woman, whose father worked at the New Toronto plant for forty-three years, whose husband joined the company at the age of nineteen and worked for thirty-six years, and whose two sons had also toiled in the Etobicoke facility, described this slap in the face as a "terrible shame." The wife of another worker said, "Our men helped build this company, but they don't even rate the same benefits as the people who work in the offices." She deplored the company treatment of "plant workers" as "second-class citizens."

Goodyear also denied severance pay to those eligible for optional early retirement, forcing them onto the (premature and lower remunerated)

David Birrell

■ **Union demonstration against Etobicoke plant closing and benefits payouts, 1987**

David Birrell

■ **NDP MPP Ruth Grier and Local 232 President David Birrell address protest, 1987.**

David Birrell

■ **NDP leader, Bob Rae, addresses Local 232 demonstration, 1987.**

pension rolls or delayed payments. The company also played games around the rate of interest it would allow on staggered benefits. Protesting workers burned Goodyear credit cards after their last shift on May 2, 1987, the wives and children of terminated workers organized three demonstrations, and a call to boycott company products went out.

Pressure was put on the Liberal government of Ontario to pass retroactive pension legislation affecting three hundred of the laid-off workers, and the union forced management into arbitration on a number of severance-and-pension-related issues, most of which resulted in rulings in its favour. John Kruger of the Pension Commission of Ontario speculated that this was going to cost Goodyear "a considerable amount of money." Toronto head office was not happy. Buzby appeared a bit beaten back: "This is just another social burden which is very nice but makes the companies that have to carry the burden on their own much less competitive," he whined. Commitments to communities and employees now went unmentioned.

Whatever the outcome of the dispute over pension and severance payments, Goodyear still came out ahead. There is no denying that almost 1,600 jobs were bartered, with state aid, for 550; that older workers were replaced by younger ones (the average age at the Napanee Goodyear plant in 1993 was thirty-one); and that a unionized workforce, with its higher wage structure secured through decades of class struggles and labour mobilization, was gutted. The hourly wages in the new plant were projected to average $13 — about $2 less than comparable figures for the organized Etobicoke factory.

As the plant doors slammed decisively shut in May 1987, and later, when the New Toronto workers discarded by Goodyear learned of the plans to build in Napanee, the smoke of Akron left an acrid taste in working-class mouths. Cory Maracle noted that if he had been able to work one more year his monthly pension would have been $975; tossed out on the street in May 1987, he received $580 after almost three decades on the Goodyear payroll. There was masculine talk of Goodyear's "cherry picking," a virginal corporate quest for fresh young labour unblemished by "the halt, the lame, and the union activists." [21] As the company spent millions of dollars expanding a plastic film manufacturing plant and, a year later, got caught out in a case of legal short-sightedness that could have cost it a $6.5-million loss on the sale of its New Toronto property, many workers no doubt regarded Goodyear's parsimonious approach to the benefits of laid-off workers as mean-spirited, to say the least.[22]

Only seventy of the more than fifteen hundred Etobicoke workers refused severance pay, opting to remain on Goodyear's recall list. Even this small number dwindled over time. "You can't live on hope," a union leader concluded. But these workers need not have bothered. Denied any special status by Goodyear, they were unacceptable, according to retired union director Vic Cosic, because they had come from the old school of unionists. Buzby explained that "everyone" had "to qualify on their own merits," and that the new Napanee production unit would almost certainly be non-union. Cosic himself was told in the company of others, by "tough cookie" Goodyear vice-president Jim Warren, "Gentlemen, we intend to keep it [Napanee] union free."[23]

Unions had been forced on Goodyear and other Akron tire giants in the mass-production mobilizations of the 1930s. But by the late 1970s and early 1980s the tide had turned against the traditional industrial strongholds of working-class organization, and Goodyear led the way in cultivating a personnel management system stripped of the awkward need to bargain collectively with working-class organizations. The United Rubber Workers of America was but one of many unions losing members in this period — its North America numbers dropping from 216,000 in 1973 to 130,000 in 1983.

Its Canadian section had never been particularly strong. Not known for militancy, the Canadian union had often been led by conservative and cautious trade unionists. At its high-water mark, the Canadian URW had only slightly more than seventeen thousand enroled in the ranks of its fifty locals, serviced by a full-time staff of only ten. In the 1970s there had been a disastrous and economically crippling attempt to unionize Nova Scotia's Michelin workers — the union is said to have spent $2 million on the failed effort. In the 1980s plant closures and worker discontent whittled down the Canadian wing to about eleven thousand members.[24]

The "Lawton Plan" was the Akron tire producer's direct response to the constraints of trade unionism, however weakened. An official company history notes that during a 1973 United Rubber Workers of America strike, Goodyear was hurt by being one of the few tire firms without a non-union plant. Convinced that the United Rubber Workers "had a long history of not settling without a strike," Akron decided to

■ **Class war from above: Rubberworkers locked out in 1983.**

get hard-nosed with its unruly workers. Returning to a Litchfieldian familialism, Goodyear opted for "tough love." It knew what was in the best interests of its workers, and it would build a new plant guided by "people motivation."

At Lawton, Oklahoma, in 1977, Goodyear erected the most modern tire plant in the world, a huge automated facility that employed eighteen hundred workers ten years later. Technology and ties to all levels of the state, from the governor down to the high school, consolidated Goodyear's Lawton success story. With a labour process under "constant computer monitoring," and with managers chosen for their proved "people orientation," productivity at Lawton soared while labour turnover, absenteeism, and accident rates dropped off precipitously. Yet workers received little in the way of increased compensation. In spite of productivity increases of 6 per cent annually over the course of the late 1980s, the paycheques of Lawton's unorganized workers registered no marked upward movement. Goodyear vice-president Stan Mihelick had a uniquely forthright statement on why wages in North American tire plants were going to stay right where they were: "Until we get real wage levels down much closer to those of the Brazils and Koreas we cannot pass along productivity gains to wages and still be competitive."[25]

Lawton was "Goodyear's first operation where factory management had absolute control of all materials and processes." It would not be the last, and its influence would not be inconsequential. The Napanee plant was to be run by Akron appointees who had served their time at Lawton. K.B. Kleckner, an "Illinois farm boy" who rose up the Goodyear ladder, would become the first Napanee plant manager after heading the Lawton operation for a part of the 1980s. His announced second-in-command, employee relations manager Paul D. Schulz, had occupied Goodyear's much-lauded "people" post at the Lawton plant from 1986 to 1988. The first Napanee-area resident to be hired to a managerial position at the new plant was a recently elected deputy reeve of Richmond Township, Tom Hogeboom, who was spirited away from a small textile firm and assigned the job of personnel manager. Almost immediately he was put on flights to Lawton and Akron. With Mihelick's views on productivity and wage levels dispersed throughout Goodyear's managerial layers, the status of unions at the Napanee plant was a foregone conclusion.[26]

The Napanee-Goodyear marriage was thus meant to be a union without trade unionism. In June 1990 Goodyear produced its first tire in Napanee; towards the end of July the company, insisting that "there are too many tires and too few buyers," announced it was laying off 360 unionized workers at its Valleyfield, Quebec, division. In the early 1980s the Valleyfield workers, long a thorn in the side of Goodyear Canada, had shifted union allegiance from the weakened United Rubber Workers to the Energy and Chemical Workers Union affiliated with the Quebec Federation of Labour. The new Local 143 embarked on a bitter nine-week strike in 1985, walking out in opposition to a company insistence on establishing a continuous seven-day work week. Eventually forced to accept Goodyear's terms, the union was intimidated by threats that the plant would be closed — threats reinforced by the removal of machinery and the discontinuance of specific production, which cost hundreds of jobs.

Cited by Goodyear Canada as the cause of its poor 1985 fiscal performance, the strike obviously strained labour-management relations at the Quebec plant to the breaking point. Five years later unionized Valleyfield would be further chastened by staggered layoffs, commencing with the cuts in late July 1990, which were followed by 530 more layoffs a month later. With the workforce slashed from 1,600 to 700, production declined from a full capacity of 21,600 tires daily to 10,000. Goodyear Canada head Samir Gibara, a recent import from Goodyear France, shed some crocodile tears. "We are very disappointed that we have to make this decision," he said with reference to the layoffs, "because we have a good and loyal workforce at Valleyfield."

But the real message was not lost on labour. The Valleyfield workers had experienced the 1985 strike defeat and the subsequent job cuts. They had heard about the 1987 closing of the unionized Etobicoke plant, the opening of the unorganized Napanee facility, a threatened job loss at a Collingwood manufacturing plant, and another Goodyear shutdown at the tire-fabric plant in St. Hyacinthe, where 144 workers were laid off in 1991. By the early 1990s, sufficiently cowed, the workers held back and class relations at Valleyfield mellowed. Employees began to be recalled in 1991-92. Lowell Dunckel, plant manager at Valleyfield, praised a "new climate on the shop floor ... improved performance in terms of price, quality, and production." Claiming waste reduction of 30-40 per cent, Dunckel was proud of getting "very good co-operation from our people." A new "breakthrough" had been achieved by "intensive talks" between plant management and union officials, who were now aware of the "competitive position" of the company and were exhibiting "a desire to do better."

"We are working together in all possible ways to insure the future of the plant," Dunckel reported. By 1992 about 370 of the more than 1,000 laid-off Valleyfield workers had returned to their wages and workplace. Goodyear spokesmen stressed that the Valleyfield and Napanee operations were now central to the well-being of the Canadian division. "Long-standing obstacles to productivity" had been overcome. The firm had a flagship non-union operation in Napanee and a well-disciplined workforce in Valleyfield, where corporate intransigence, a willingness to play hardball in its capacity to shut down production completely, and well-timed use of the pink slip had taught unruly unionized workers who was truly the boss.[27]

From Lawton to Valleyfield, with the dismantling of Etobicoke/New Toronto thrown in for good measure, the recent history of Goodyear wrote unionism decisively out of the company's picture of production in Napanee. Inspired by the staunch and successful anti-unionism of its Nova Scotia-based rival, Michelin, which had beat back a series of inept union drives by the rubberworkers in the 1970s, Goodyear had no intention of allowing organized labour so much as a toehold in its new flagship plant. "Napanee clearly surpasses the technological resources of our competitors," claimed Canadian president Gibara in 1990. "In the struggle for market dominance, which will become an all-out war this decade, Napanee has positioned us to leap ahead of the competition ... forging ahead in the marketplace."

Trade unionism had no place in this corporate vision. The United Rubber, Cork, Linoleum and Plastics Workers of America managed to get some two dozen workers at the new Napanee facility interested in the union in 1990-91. Many of these signed union cards and provided information to the Toronto-based union. A secret meeting was called, with union officials travelling to Napanee. Only seven workers showed up, two of whom were unknown to the organizers. On the very day of the "secret meeting" Goodyear announced a wage hike of 4.5 per cent. The company made sure it had spies among the unionists, scuttled this original organizing effort, and effectively threw cold water on the rather tepid URW forays into Napanee.

After being received with disinterest during a singular leafleting effort in 1991, the union withdrew and largely conceded that Goodyear would, in all likelihood, remain free of trade unionism. By 1993 barely a dozen Goodyear workers were still linked, however tenuously, to the shrinking Toronto-based URW. While left-leaning Local 232 president David Birrell says he still wants to see the Napanee plant organized before he dies, the more conservative Vic Cosic, one-time Canadian director of the URW, has concluded that workers at Goodyear believe they "don't need a union." They supposedly feel at home in the Goodyear family.

This turn of events would no doubt please Scott Buzby, who confessed in 1988: "When we start up any plant, of course, we want to have a free hand to be able to establish the work systems and the flexibility. So that's what we do.... We want a union between us and our people — that's the type of union we want."[28]

B. Spremo/ *Toronto Star*

■ **The final fall:**
Dynamiting Goodyear's Etobicoke smokestack.

Chapter Eight

Celebrating Corporatism:
Bread, Circuses, and the Blimp

By Akron standards, the announcement of Goodyear's intention to build in Napanee was low key. The cloak of secrecy was lifted in late March 1988 as Goodyear executives moved to deflect the rumours and "leaks" of their eastern Ontario plans. An even dozen company representatives came — "incognito in a standard brown van"— to the town on March 25 and met with members of the business community, regional politicians, and journalists — eighty in all — at a local banquet hall. "Hi, we're Goodyear," they said. They then paid their visit to the Napanee District Secondary School, where the focus was on thanking the students for their spirited co-operation and enthusiastic pitch for jobs.

A month and a half later the tire plant was officially "blessed" at a private luncheon in Toronto with Ontario Premier David Peterson and Keith MacDonald and Hugh O'Neil, local members of the provincial legislature (MPPs). Hours later Monte Kwinter, Ontario's new minister of industry, trade, and technology, announced the financial details in the provincial parliament. At about the same time Napanee officials got word from Akron via a conference call.[1]

With a prenuptial agreement settling the property and labour force issues pretty much nailed down, Goodyear saw the moment as overripe for a gala celebratory event. The marriage of Napanee and Goodyear would be consummated with a breathtaking extravaganza, with Goodyear footing a "bride price" bill of over $100,000 for a mid-July sod-turning ceremony. "Bread and circuses" were coming to town, and the Goodyear Blimp, known as The America, was on its way.[2]

Promoted as the "largest corporate symbol in the world," The America was built in 1982 at a cost of $2.8 million. One of three such corporate dirigibles, the blimp was named after the yacht that won the America's Cup Race in 1951. An imposing 192 feet in length, 50 feet

Whig Standard

■ **Napanee Mayor Harold Webster at the March 1988 announcement banquet.**

wide, and 59 feet high, the oversized balloon is powered by twin 210-horsepower engines, maintained by almost 205,000 cubic feet of helium, and can reach a maximum speed of 50 miles an hour. Goodyear first built blimps during World War I, when they were used as coastal surveillance vehicles by the U.S. Navy. Drawn to the "eye-catching" possibilities, the company adapted an essentially wartime technology into its project of symbolic self-promotion. With limited carrying capacity — six passengers in the gondola — the Goodyear blimps are a labour-intensive item. Each of them requires a ground crew of twenty-two (five pilots, sixteen crew members, and one public relations officer). Their flights are monitored twenty-four hours a day by a convoy of vehicles. Most rides — and all the rides that took place that month at Napanee — are by invitation only: eight thousand passengers annually get the corporate-sponsored "sensation of a lifetime."[3] For The America to make the trip from Houston, the Napanee-Goodyear party obviously ranked high with Akron's head office.

Scheduled for July 13, 5:00 P.M. at the town fairgrounds, Goodyear's final promotional blowout was billed as the Napanee-Goodyear Friendship Festival. The company hired a twenty-seven-year-old Napanee resident, Tracy Trottier, who had first contacted Goodyear Canada's public relations director, Peter Rose, when she was co-ordinating Kingston's annual Cheese and Fine Food Festival and searching for corporate sponsors. Several months later Rose offered Trottier a unique job: organize a party for ten thousand people.

Starting June 17 she got down to basics. There were meetings with town administrators, police and emergency personnel, caterers, service clubs, and media outlets. The Goodyear officials she met with assured her that money was no object. But they were adamant about certain details: the dozens of cars and limousines rented for the event, for instance, had to be running on Goodyear tires. Napanee recreation director Brenda Andress became Trottier's "right arm," helping with those areas — such as the forty portable toilets — that Goodyear left to her discretion. Trottier dropped in to NDSS, where she found twenty students to work on the renovations to the Napanee Fair Grounds.

When she wasn't confirming hotel reservations for incoming Goodyear dignitaries, attending to security provisions, or making sure the 12,500 Goodyear caps, 20,000 blimp-shaped balloons, tens of thousands of stickers, streamers, and flags, or 30,000 custom-made Goodyear coffee cups were properly locked up in the fairground's arena, Trottier was fielding questions from local residents, who dropped in to offer Goodyear congratulations or express their fears about how the company was going to alter the future of the town. Trottier was bullish on Goodyear, an enthusiasm she attributed to a community-spirited upbringing on a local farm: "Napanee deserves standing applause. The local pride here is really strong and everybody realizes how important it is to pull this thing together and show Goodyear what we're capable of. Everyone's so excited and keyed up here.... There's a really strong sense of community."

Curiously, Trottier had managed to turn her job into proving to Goodyear that Napanee warranted the company expenditure. At the same time she could view the festivities as "a thank-you to the Napanee area."[4] As community and company approached the altar, both apparently needed reassurances that the marriage would work.

Behind the scenes, however, those who had arranged the union were making a party-within-a-party. A VIP dinner at the curling club brought together the important inner circle, with Trottier looking after matters of corporate and political protocol, deciding who ranked foremost: a federal cabinet minister or the premier of the province. Concerned to touch all material bases, Goodyear's guest list for the dinner included both federal and provincial politicians and cabinet members, an assortment of civil servants, and, finally, "all the who's who of Napanee." Goodyear itself was represented by Robert E. Mercer, Chairman of the Board of Directors, Scott Buzby, Canadian President and C.E.O., fourteen officials from Akron, and ninety employees from the company's Toronto offices. By the July 13 date the guest list had grown to four hundred, and six hundred cars with VIP stickers clogged the choice sites near the fairgrounds, necessitating the creation of another parking lot for the rest of the privileged.[5]

By the second week of July Napanee was in high gear for the Goodyear "friendship fest." Local merchants came up with $2,000 to mount a week-long corporate photo display for the incoming company, and downtown Napanee shops were draped with "Welcome Goodyear" signs. Businesses and organizations took out advertisements in the local newspaper, while community officials adopted a rhetoric of historical comparison. Napanee mayor Harold Webster thought the Goodyear arrival in Napanee was "probably the most important day ... in its 124-year history." North Fredericksburgh's reeve Don McCabe declared, "Goodyear is the greatest thing that has happened to Napanee since Confederation."

The local detachment of the Ontario Provincial Police had their minds on other matters. They feared "the biggest traffic jam in the world" and announced that they would be posting a six-person R.I.D.E team to monitor those who might be tempted to drink at their homes or cottages and drive in "just to see the blimp." Out-of-town visitors were urged to park at local schools, while Napanee residents were encouraged to walk or view the blimp and night fireworks from afar.[6]

Ostensibly a sod-turning ceremony to sanctify the building of the new tire plant, the July 13 event had only the most tenuous symbolic connection to an actual ground-breaking. Goodyear had no desire to have thousands of people traipse across the back lots of its recently acquired property, and it would have been difficult to orchestrate a celebratory party on the undeveloped land. So the company came up with a novel plan, one that fit well with its focused imagery of down-home familialism. Promising to bring the sod-turning to the people, rather than the people to the sod-turning, Goodyear announced: "We're not doing the ground breaking at the plant site because we

WEDNESDAY, JULY 13 at 6 o'clock, we're having a party to celebrate the ground breaking of the new Goodyear Napanee plant. Bring your family and all your friends to the Napanee Fair Grounds to join the Goodyear–Napanee Friendship Festival celebrations. We're planning lots of fun and games for everyone, including ice cream and cake, fireworks, games and prizes. And, of course, the Goodyear blimp will be in attendance! So come on down to the Napanee Fair Grounds and help ring in the Goodyear!

GOODYEAR·NAPANEE
Friendship Festival

Napanee Beaver

■ **Above: Friendship Festival Announcement**

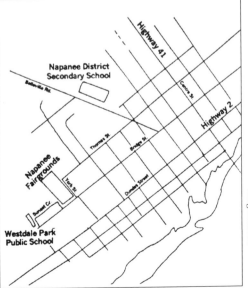

Whig Standard

■ **Below: Festival Parking Map**

want to reflect the plant belongs to the town and the area." Instead of local dignitaries wielding golden shovels at the actual construction site, they would be feted at the VIP dinner and treated to special daytime rides in the Goodyear blimp.

For the ceremony itself, the company transported truckloads of dirt from the factory's future location and built "the world's biggest sandbox" (40 by 60 feet) on a stage at the Napanee Fair Grounds. About two hundred local children from five regional schools, aged eight to twelve, were selected by lot and the permission of their parents secured. Outfitted with shovels and pails, dressed in white Goodyear garb, the children would break the ground of the new plant before the huge crowd, searching for seven hundred special corporate medallions buried in the sandbox. The medallions could be redeemed for prizes, including rides in the blimp. Goodyear spokespersons made the most of this popular public relations ploy, stressing the "memorable and non-traditional" nature of the ceremonial sod-turning, which was also fittingly a treasure hunt for the young who would figure so strongly in the marriage of company and community.

Peter Rose emphasized this carefully chosen act of representation, stressing the innovative corporate effort to symbolically link company, community, and childhood, all of which now had a future. "We wanted to be innovative, and to represent as much of the community as possible — and to symbolize the future," he said, and he went on to emphasize that many of the children in the hunt would eventually be working for the company. More than a hundred NDSS students were hand-picked by Rod Hughes and Barney O'Connor, who quickly and co-operatively responded to Goodyear's request for volunteer workers. Students in the targeted industrial physics classes and members of the seemingly company-friendly Students Council were given the first opportunity to make themselves available. NDSS student leaders Mark Arsenault and Nancy Gilbert were chosen to introduce the children's sandbox sod-breaking by pulling the plunger on glittering skyrockets and hundreds of red, white, and blue balloons.[7]

Corporate promotional campaigns of the sort Goodyear envisioned for Napanee on July 13 sometimes fall flat. In the case of the Goodyear-Napanee Friendship Festival, the celebration surpassed the expectations of even the most optimistic company boosters. Kicking things off was a late afternoon press conference featuring the political dignitaries, who arrived, for the most part, in gleaming white stretch limousines. But the real statement of the day was to come from the local citizenry themselves.

A massive crowd thronged to the fairgrounds, and less than an hour after the formal festivities began at six o'clock they had devoured an entire eight-by-four-foot, one thousand-piece cake, as well as 125 smaller cakes, along with tons of ice cream and watermelon and hundreds of cases of soft drinks. Some twelve thousand Goodyear caps disappeared in a matter of minutes, and six thousand rain checks were handed out. It seems there was some hoarding of the "freebies." Early arrivals were seen marching triumphantly to their parked cars with stacks of the give-away headgear. One boastful grandmother claimed to have scored fifty-three Goodyear caps. An entrepreneurial child was reputedly hawking the hats for three dollars, displaying an individualism and initiative that, for the party moment, was out of step with the desired imagery of Goodyear-Napanee co-operation.

But the real problem was that of a bloated marketplace: demand exceeded supply. Expecting between five thousand and ten thousand, Goodyear faced a human deluge of more than twenty thousand people pouring onto a fairgrounds used to servicing a town with a total population of less than one-quarter that number. The celebrants came from Gananoque, Kingston, Belleville, Trenton — points east and west along the 401 highway — as well as from countless small towns and villages to the north. And they kept coming. For the children there were pony rides, a petting zoo, and face painting; for senior citizens there were special seating arrangements near the stage. The continuous entertainment featured country and western music, area fiddlers and step-dancers, NDSS bands, and local choirs. Shortly after seven o'clock public relations manager Rose shook his head in surprise: "Our last count was 20,000. It's unbelievable. This is the biggest event we've had in Canada for sure — without a doubt." John Luna of Toronto's Multiple Images Limited, videotaping the proceedings for Goodyear's corporate technological scrapbook, called the celebration "the Woodstock of Napanee."[8]

Luna mistook form for content. Woodstock was an expression of the commercialized but essentially countercultural anti-establishment ethos of 1960s youth. The Goodyear-Napanee Friendship Festival was an example of conscious corporate, capitalist self-promotion. Company executives knew the price they were paying was small indeed for the social and economic dividends they would reap at a later date. Goodyear chairman Mercer acknowledged that the money expended was in actuality an investment in future corporate-community relations. It was expected to boost morale and solidify the image of the company as a caring, public-spirited citizen. "While there's been a modest investment with this party," he noted, "the return on that investment will be that the plant will get started faster and quality levels will be achieved quicker with an *esprit de corps* in the community.... You can't put a dollar and cents sign on the benefits it brings in morale, productivity, quality, and enjoyment." Scott Buzby indicated that the extravagant company blowout was meant to induce those people who were not on the playing field with Goodyear to come on down out of the bleachers and "get into the scrum."[9]

Metaphors of competitive winning "teamwork" were indeed commonplace at the party. Addressing the crowd just before dusk, Mercer said, "As I look out here, it looks to me as if everyone's a member of the team, and I like that. In fact, Napanee seems to be a city of champions." Mayor Webster led the crowd in a "team spirit" cheer: "Give me a G ... Give me an O ... Give me another O ..." Premier Peterson called Goodyear a world-class competitor whose project was a "win-win situation" for all concerned. His minister of industry, trade, and technology declared that Goodyear was "a true world-beater in the tire industry." For plant manager K.B. Kleckner, class relations were not at all metaphorical, and he took the chance to extol the new ground that would soon be broken by Goodyear's "team" approach to production.

And then, speeches done, the children scrambled for the "Goodyear *gold*," dust swirling on stage as the sod-breaking quest for corporate prizes began. Even those children who came up empty, at least on this day of "friendship," got a token token and did not have to go home empty-handed. With darkness approaching, the blimp America hovered overhead, surrounded by balloons, its 7,500 lights joined by more than eighty miles of wire flashing out a "Super Skytacular" show. The four-hour event, consistently hailed as featuring the world's "biggest" and "best," culminated in a spectacular $25,000 fireworks display rivalling "anything ever seen before in the area."[10]

If seeing is indeed believing, eastern Ontario witnessed a corporate love-in on the 13th of July. There were the odd voices of dissent, but they were strangely dissonant, distanced from the devotion of the main-

Whig Standard

■ Letting them eat cake:
Crowds line up in the Napanee arena for various hand-outs.

Whig Standard

■ Goodyear Youth:
Tracy Trottier coaches 200 children "ground breakers"

Whig Standard

■ Goodyear's blimp,
The America, over
Napanee.

■ $25,000 goes up
in smoke

Whig Standard

stream and drowned in the din of economic expectation. Questioning the coming of Goodyear was akin to interrogating motherhood or standing firm against progress. Basically it just wasn't done. Trade unionism failed to rear its head in protest; the conservative officialdom of the United Rubber Workers apparently thought it was inappropriate to leaflet the event on behalf of the laid-off Etobicoke workers. Vic Cosic drove down to Napanee after an "informal" managerial invitation, but the Local 232 leader, the more militant David Birrell, scoffed at the Friendship Festival. "Gee, I thought I would've gotten a gold-embossed invite," he mocked, adding in sober afterthought: "No, we weren't expecting any ... we're still waiting for $3 million worth of severance pay for some of our guys."

Even those who raised their eyebrows in the aftermath of the Friendship Festival did so with reluctance or with the acknowledgement that their views were likely to find few takers. Larry South, Liberal MPP for Frontenac-Addington, assured one and all he was pro-Goodyear and did not want to "rain on anyone's parade" when he sounded a nationalist note of disapproval. He said that the Goodyear blimp could have been renamed "Airship Canada" for a day. One naysayer, Harvey Schachter of the Kingston *Whig-Standard* editorial board, chastized the corporate waste involved in the megaparty, suggesting that the money spent could better have gone to assist the community food bank, welfare recipients, or physical improvements in public services that would be needed because of the local growth associated with Goodyear's coming to town. He said that a company so lucratively on the take with the state might be a little less free with the taxpayer dollars that had recently come its way. But he recognized that few politicians, basking "in the joy of delivering jobs," would see things in this negative light.

Schachter pointed to an irony in the situation. The universal success of Goodyear in captivating Napanee was the very reason the company did not need to engage in a "needlessly expensive extravaganza":

And now, after those financial manoeuvres, the company — flush with government handouts — is hosting a sod-turning to beat all sod-turnings. The event will be a vital aspect of Goodyear's public relations program — even though Napanee, currently, is the last place the company needs to spend money on public relations, since virtually everybody there adores the company providing the long-awaited economic boost.

Some local residents wondered aloud if the town was now going to grow too big and impersonal — fears quickly dismissed by most of the "party-goers," who welcomed the jobs and possibilities for youth that Goodyear seemed to guarantee. A father of three grown children, all of whom had moved to industrial centres to secure work, summed up the consensus: "Napanee was kind of a retirement town, and this is going to change things." Goodyear's coming, he thought, would give the kids something to stay in town for. "It's the best thing that's happened around here in at least a decade," another resident said. "It will be especially good for the young people."

Teased with the question, "How do you like the smell of burning rubber?" a farmer near the Goodyear site who also happened to own a local General Motors dealership replied, "Just fine." When asked if she had any concerns about the plant, one working-class woman with a foundry-worker husband answered curtly, "I can't imagine what worries there could be." For their part, Goodyear's Toronto head-office visitors nuzzled up to the quaint cosiness of Napanee, playing on a local sense of superiority to "the Big City." "I like the quiet and the simplicity of it here," one of them said. "It's not like the hustle and bustle of Toronto where everything goes so fast you have to hold on to your false eyelashes."[11]

Of course, nobody wants to cry in anguish and protest at a wedding, especially when the bride and groom seem locked in the embrace of economic bliss, sanctioned by the values of godly higher authority. Goodyear Canada's Buzby rang the matrimonial bells loudly and unambiguously in his speech to the huge throng. "It's just like a country wedding here," he enthused. "The good Lord must be looking after all of us." His Akron colleague Bob Mercer concurred: "This is a full church wedding."[12] Paul W. Litchfield, who had headed Goodyear when Mercer began his ascent up the corporate ladder in the 1940s, would have been proud of what his "boys" had accomplished in Napanee.

After the crowd dispersed, Goodyear's volunteer "team" of NDSS students and others laboured until two in the morning cleaning the fairgrounds and the arena. The next evening a grateful Goodyear threw a private party for seventy of the students at the Napanee Arena. It began with a barbecue dinner and presentations of Goodyear racing jackets and T-shirts graced with the blimp and emblazoned with the self-congratulatory statement "WE DID IT!" Some of those hired on for three weeks of fence repair, painting, and general clean-up received a "salary" of approximately $370, but most worker volunteers got Goodyear's thanks and mementos of the company-community festival. With these in tow they danced the night away to the music of The Flamingos, a Kingston-area band.

"The world is watching us and we want everybody to know it," Mercer had explained when asked why the event needed to be such a huge undertaking. "We have backed into a few towns in the past in the still of the night. But everybody loses that way." Goodyear consciously cultivated a sense of victory through its launching of the Friendship Festival party. It *was* bread and circuses, but for most of those in attendance it seemed to strike the right note of festive optimism. Wives and workers, retired pensioners, and young boys and girls: most agreed that July 13 was a day to remember. "We've lived here all of our lives," said a fifty-year-old hospital worker, "and we've never seen anything like this and probably never will again." For an elderly woman, Goodyear's extravaganza "put Napanee on the map." Her unambiguous assessment was: "It's super ... a wonderful show."[13]

Writing in the *Napanee Beaver*, in a special postground-breaking edition headed "FRIENDS FOREVER," Maxine Hagerman spelled out in journalistic hyperbole the message Akron executives wanted to see and hear. July 13 was "an excitement-filled event like none the area [had] ever experienced before"; the fireworks display was "climactic and truly awesome"; the party itself was "virtually flawless." Hagerman thanked the volunteers and workers who made it all possible, but she saved the ultimate credit and "biggest thanks" for that "good old wingfoot express." Goodyear executives were "*people* people," who would, she felt, "blend in perfectly with the community."

For Hagerman, "Wednesday evening was the beginning of something very big — something which will entail a lifetime of friendship between this terrific area and the Goodyear family." Goodyear, she said, deserved "a million thanks."[14]

After the sod-busting there were a few sober reminders that life is not just a party. The event was all image-making, an important chance for Goodyear to represent its own brand of corporate familialism, wedded to team spirit and community values. But winning in the world was not so much a symbolic act for the men from Akron as it was a matter of production and profit. Mercer and other Goodyear executives revelled in the effusive rhetoric of the Friendship Festival, but they had no illusions about why they were there in Napanee. "We break ground here today for the most advanced radial passenger tire production facility in the world," Mercer said in one of his drier moments. "The difference it makes will change the face of the tire industry."

As Napanee and its environs recovered from the fun and the excited, exhibitionistic displays of "friendship" featured throughout the festivities, town boomers got back to basics. A *Beaver* editorial noted that many walked the streets "in zombie-like fashion" subsequent to the Goodyear blowout, while others could be seen after July 13 "wearily slumping at their desks." The paper noted, "Hushed silences seemed to be filling some area workplaces on Thursday," but took pains not to be too critical of what seemed a lethargic let-down: "Such excitement all at one time took its toll on Napaneans. But the fun and friendship made all of the post-party exhaustion well worth it."

It was apparently a relief "to have all of the hype" over with. Napanee had gone through months of suspense before the mystery firm concluded its clandestine business dealings; weeks of tense disappointment had followed as the anonymous firm seemed ready to pull back in the face of bottoms falling out of property packages; then there was a time trial in which the town waited for the state to deliver on Goodyear's economic demands. When the official announcement did eventually come, it had been followed by a gala celebration. Now, "It's time to really get the tire rolling, to get that plant built and staffed, and to get those tires to a very demanding market." The work ahead constituted nothing less than another "great challenge which is sure to revitalize a town which in a lot of ways has sat stagnant over the last 10 or 15 years." It was time to get "into gear with Goodyear."[15] The Akron multinational had let the town eat cake. Now it was back to business. Public promotions gave way to private development.

Chapter Nine

The Costs of Construction:
Building the World's Most Modern Tire Plant

In many ways Goodyear's invasion of Napanee ended with the July 13 Friendship Festival. What followed, with the actual physical construction of the plant, employment of workers, and production of tires, was somewhat anti-climactic. Once established in Napanee, its hold over the community comfortably secure, Goodyear settled into the actualities of production in a quiet, matter-of-fact way. To be sure, the building, paid employment, and output of the new Goodyear facility — as the material substance of a steel-reinforced presence in the Napanee region — can hardly be ignored. But in the colonization of the community, important dimensions of Goodyear's work had been accomplished well before the profitable edifice of output began to take on concrete shape.

The Goodyear invasion of Napanee is particularly noteworthy, then, because it indicates the importance of establishing ideological hegemony and sustaining a kind of cultural imperialism as capitalism penetrates its own, once marginalized, hinterlands. With its acquisition of property, its unmistakable integration of the structures of local government and education into the project of capitalist "development," and its pressuring of state authority and the possibility of trade union resistance into postures of compliant acquiescence, Goodyear was engaged in a massive hegemonic act of primitive accumulation that set the stage for the actual construction and, later, production of its imposing plant. Once established as a physical object, with respect to jobs and economic survival in the backcountry Goodyear's Napanee factory would continue to build, ideologically and culturally, on the gains and accomplishments and definitions of human need that had been central in the unfolding events of 1987 and 1988.

If imperialism is indeed the highest stage of capitalism, our understanding of imperialism within a late capitalism that has penetrated —

militarily and economically — all corners of the globe perhaps needs to shift ground. Rather, we need to appreciate a new imperialism, concentrated not on the Third World — however much a site of imperialist activity that may be — but on the underdeveloped peripheries and marginal regional enclaves of unevenly developed but economically advanced nation-states.[1] To be sure, this new imperialism, and the export of capital entailed, are product-specific, and commodities such as tires are ideally suited to the intra-capitalist economies of relocation. Tires are tied to the more advanced sectors of capitalist consumption, both in terms of their relationship to the sparkling products of GM, Ford, Chrysler, Honda, and Toyota, as well as through their importance in replacement markets, which are bound to be more expansive in North America than in the Third World, where nothing is discarded — "bits of Coca-Cola bottles and Goodyear tires and chamber pots," in the words of one Nicaraguan poet — that cannot be patched or padded, pieced back together with a resilient ingenuity now long absent in the affluent economies of the privileged west.[2]

The building of the Napanee plant coincided with Goodyear's aggressive movement into the replacement tire market. This was consolidated in acquisitions of western Canadian retail and distribution outlets and a conscious marketing choice to accentuate not only tire sales but also automotive service. Culminating in the highly successful "We Market More Than Tires" advertising campaign, featuring Los Angeles comic Thom Sharpe, Goodyear's strategy since the late 1980s has been to capture more and more of the consumer dollars associated with cars and their upkeep. When Goodyear acquired Manitoba-based York Tire in 1988, picking up fifteen retail outlets, four warehouses, and two retread plants, a tire industry figure noted, "There's been a sort of war, really more of a competition, going on among tire manufacturers to increase their share of the market." Goodyear intended to win this war of competition. Building on the firm's reputation as a tire producer, it hardened up exclusive retailing commitments, expanded service outlets, opened a mechanic training centre in Toronto, and started promoting new tire technologies.[3]

Goodyear may thus epitomize the extent to which capitalism's much-heralded new global reach is not solely about the dramatic shift in capitalist production to Mexico, Korea, and Taiwan. To be sure, Akron's tire kings have every intention of continuing to exploit the possibilities of the Third World, especially the expansive Asian market; by the late 1980s South Korea had already been targeted as the next Goodyear venture. But capital's late twentieth-century restructuring is also about the recolonization of capitalist "backwaters," within which intensified managerial "freedoms" can be cultivated in the late twentieth century. And there remain sufficiently lucrative North American "Fordist" markets that firms such as Goodyear see as viable sources of profit. This registered over the course of the 1970s and 1980s in a process of global restructuring of the tire industry. At least thirty-seven North American plants closed their doors in those years, with many of the shutdowns coming in the long-established centres of heavy industry such as Akron, Detroit, Los Angeles, Toronto, and Hamilton. This put almost thirty-four thousand largely unionized rubberworkers out of their jobs.[4]

There were also other corporate liquidations. At the same time that Goodyear contemplated building a new plant in Napanee it was finalizing the sale of its Kinshasa tire-making unit, Goodyear Zaire Sarl. Two years later, with construction in Napanee under way, the Akron-based firm quit its forty-two-year-old South African operations. Citing the impossibility of obtaining "adequate returns on investment" due to anti-apartheid sanctions and the slide in the world standing of the rand, Goodyear sold off its Uitenhage tire and rubber plant to Anglovaal, a mining and industrial group. The largely black and "coloured" workforce, 2,400 strong, were supposedly not to lose their jobs, and the new owners were touted as attentive to human rights. Yet at the very moment that Goodyear announced the sale, the South African motor vehicle industry was in the midst of five weeks of strikes involving some thirteen thousand members of the National Union of Metalworkers of South Africa, crippling production in two-thirds of the auto sector. The twelve hundred Goodyear employees defying corporate will were immediately told that if they did not accept the employment conditions proposed by the new South African management they would be fired.[5]

Compared to the turmoil posed for Goodyear in South Africa, where by the late 1980s class and race had combined to create a volatile context of protest, and where the climate of production and profit was constantly clouded, placid non-union eastern Ontario no doubt seemed a hospitable environment for a beleaguered capital. The colonization of the region, moreover, had already been accomplished, indeed welcomed. It is surely not insignificant that local Napanee youth, drawing on a reservoir of social chauvinism and racism, as well as cynicism and hostility to Goodyear's managerial reification of the concept of "team" consciousness and activity, refer to the new tire facility as "the Jap plant."[6] To them, imperialism has come home.

The summer of 1990 was a good season for Goodyear. With the new eastern Ontario plant gearing up for its much anticipated productive baptism, the multinational was expecting a second-quarter profit. But typical of the company's now-established low-key presence in Napanee, there was none of the hoopla of 1988. Phase One of Goodyear's construction plans were completed, the 600,000 square-foot factory stretching out to about one kilometre in length, occupying a space the equivalent of thirteen football fields. Tires had been in production since early in the year, a staged process in which the first radial pushed off the line on January 25 was somewhat experimental and flawed. Two months later the plant was producing quality tires, but was still largely dependent on components shipped in from outside sources. Finally, on June 25, all of the bugs had been ironed out and Napanee's plant produced its first "home-grown" independent radial tire.

Daily output rose quickly from two thousand to four thousand and was initially stockpiled and then shipped to the replacement-tire market of Goodyear service dealers. One-third of the computerized tire-making machines were up and running, some having been purchased and imported from Asia, their installation supervised by a group of Japanese engineers who conducted ceremonial Buddhist blessings, splashing the new technology with wine to the surprise of plant manager K.B. Kleckner. To commemorate all of this the company had a modest flag-raising ceremony outside the plant, as Kleckner, Indianapolis 500 driver Scott Goodyear (no relation to the firm, but a human symbol of safety connected directly to quality tires), and a handful of corporate officials gathered in front of the factory. Kleckner expressed satisfaction about having worked "on a facility design for more than three years and finally coming to a point where the machines are functional." But he stressed that his job was far from done. "It will be another one-and-a-half years before we're up to capacity of 14,000 tires per day."

Journalists stressed the mundane nature of the event, "a simple and concise ceremony." One reported, "There was no fanfare, no blimp America. Thousands of balloons didn't drop from the air, nor did kids line up for hours for commemorative hats like they did for the 1988 party."[7] It was almost as though Kleckner and his bosses, having won the hearts and minds of Napanee on the whirlwind courtship and honeymoon of an early period, now wanted to settle down to the *routine* of *private*, propertied family life. Goodyear no longer needed to be in the public eye.

Kleckner joked that the first tire off the line had cost $320 million — the price of plant investment. True to corporate form, he enjoyed noting that the second one had come into the world with its costs cut in half.[8] But there were other prices to be paid in building the world's most modern radial tire plant, costs measured not in dollars and cents but in livelihoods and actual lives.

When construction began on the new facility in 1988, Goodyear continued to promote Napanee as a town where "the people are good, stable workers and they participate in their community." In the "fiercely competitive tire industry," state-of-the-art technology had to be complemented by "a comparable work ethic." Akron head office chose Napanee to be "the new jewel in ... Goodyear Canada's crown ... the most modern, technologically advanced facility of its kind in the world" because its people "provided the personal philosophy that is required in a team-oriented, employee-involved operation." As Goodyear screened applications for jobs through the local "hiring halls" — Canada Employment Centre and NDSS — it scrutinized potential production workers through gruelling sets of interviews, totalling twenty-six hours, leaving nothing to chance in its quest for workers governed by the ostensible "Napanee philosophy."

It was rumoured that prospective Goodyear employees were interviewed three to four times, and only one in ten who went through the interview process landed a job. Much of the interrogation turned on responding to questions as a "proper team member," and applicants who got to this stage of the interview (but were ultimately unsuccessful) remember the pseudo-psychologism of Goodyear. It was apparently like being trapped between the pages of *Psychology Today*. Finally, if candidates did make it this far down the Goodyear hiring line they were required, in step with Goodyear's familialism but possibly in violation of the Human Rights Code and various government guidelines around appropriate hiring procedures, to be accompanied by a spouse or parent, who was also questioned. Essentially wives and parents were asked if they, too, could measure up to the requirements of being "team members." Most people are born into families; Goodyear was choosing its extended kinship network and telling prospective relatives that they had better be able to adapt to life in the new clan. Months of training were then capped with an eight-week introduction to the Goodyear system as potential hirees were shipped off to plants such as Lawton to familiarize themselves with the environment of advanced tire production.

Goodyear Napanee's Shelley Aylesworth-Spink confirmed, "It is not easy to be hired by the Goodyear factory. There are a whole bunch of things they have to jump through before they are offered the position." This contrasted sharply with prior "training" at the Etobicoke/New Toronto plant. Dave Birrell, who worked twenty-three years for Goodyear and later became president of what remained of the once twelve-hundred-strong Local 232 of the United Rubber, Cork, Linoleum and Plastic Workers of America, recalls now that when he was hired a manager looked you over, sized you up, and sent you into the factory. Tire machinery, Birrell says, did not require a PhD to operate. You learned on the job. A retired union official wondered aloud why Goodyear was demanding that all prospective hirees have Grade 12 education when such schooling had absolutely no relationship to many of the available jobs. Workers with past union experience and the many disgruntled youth and established tradesmen, women, and labourers who failed to secure employment came to refer to Goodyear's marathon interview sessions and extensive training program as "brainwashing."[9]

Those who managed to secure jobs were fed a steady diet of Goodyear imagery and rhetoric that continued where the interview and selection process left off. The in-house

APPLICATION DAY
▼
ORIENTATION
▼
JOB FIT & GATB TEST
▼
SCREENING INTERVIEW
▼
ASSESSMENT CENTRE
▼
FINAL INTERVIEW
▼
REFERENCE CHECK
▼
PRE-EMPLOYMENT ORIENTATION
▼
JOB OFFER
▼
HEALTH EXAM

newspaper at the Napanee plant, *Tire Tracks*, began to promote specific cherished themes: one issue depicts clasped hands representative of the Goodyear/Napanee District Secondary School, the corporate-educational unity appearing under the headline, "The real world." Stickers and slogans stress safety and quality, while a seminar notebook cover offers a uniquely entrepreneurial conception of balanced relations. Resting on a cylinder composed of Business Plans, Systems Organization, Strategy, Vision, Philosophy, and Objective is a "tri-balanced" ordering of the needs

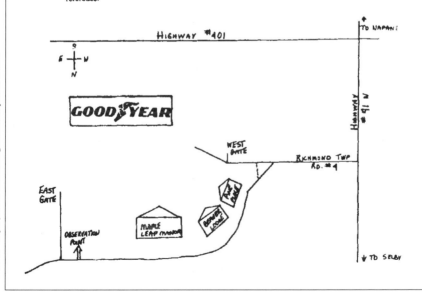

■ Left and Above: The selection process

of business, customers, and team members. To the materialist cynic, profit might appear to be the core of this carefully balanced fulcrum, but it is nowhere to be seen among the named purposes of production.[10]

By mid-January 1989 the actual building of the plant was well under way. The foundations were laid, 60 per cent of the structural steel work completed, and roofing and siding proceeding apace. By February Goodyear had hired six contractors to work on various aspects of construction and had ten more contracts left to negotiate. Each contract carried a value of $2 million to $3 million.[11]

Nicholas Rogers

■ **Team members come first**

More was at stake, however, than mere money. Early on Goodyear's general contractor, BOT Construction of Oakville, became embroiled in a dispute involving Kingston-based Local 249 of the International Carpenters' Union and the Kingston and Belleville locals of the International Laborers Union and the Operating Engineers Union. Picket-lines appeared at the Goodyear site on September 23, 1988, with the carpenters protesting that BOT was bringing in workers from outside the region, employing non-union labour, and using general labourers to make forms for the plant foundations, a job the Carpenters' Union considered properly the sphere of its own members. With a detachment of the Ontario Provincial Police in attendance, the understated calm Goodyear wanted for the building of the plant dissipated. One protesting tradesman was arrested for striking a vehicle as it was ushered through the picket-line by police. As the BOT owners denied the union allegations of wrongdoing, placing the blame for the "misunderstanding" on a dispute between two labour bodies and insisting they were hiring through local union halls and subcontracting work with regional firms, Goodyear obviously wanted the tension diffused. A Goodyear official attended an informal meeting between the disputants, but most union officials, and certainly BOT, agreed that the company was not involved in the controversy.

One disgruntled carpenter said, "Goodyear knew very well what they were doing when they awarded BOT the general contract. You have to wonder if this is an indication of what sort of corporate citizen Goodyear is going to be." He concluded, "I don't think it bodes very well for their future if they are going to be the cause of this sort of labor trouble right at the outset." Eventually settled through a series of local meetings and finally resolved in negotiations between the two Toronto-based unions, the Goodyear brush with organized labour was hardly a serious and sustained eruption of class struggle. But it signalled precisely the kind of "interference" that Goodyear had no intention of tolerating.[12]

Neil Ward

■ **Countenances of class, I**

Photos: Neil Ward

■ **Countenances of class, II**

■ Running the gauntlet, I

■ Running the gauntlet, II

Neil Ward

■ **Backing the state**

However minimal the labour dispute at the Goodyear construction site, it did present the countenance of working-class organization, long obscured by the ideology and aesthetics of a finances-driven familialism. As Neil Ward's photographs make clear, whatever the weakened state of labour in these times, class still exists as potential opposition in advanced capitalist societies, even in contexts, such as that of Goodyear-Napanee, in which much has been done to stifle and silence it. Class can still mount a challenge, forcing those who would deny its existence to run particular kinds of gauntlets and draw on old protections. Appearing at dawn, shadowed by the police arm of the state, class power did surface at the Goodyear site, if only to put in a token appearance as Goodyear contractors undertook to transform the ideas and images of the wingfoot clan into a sprawling architecture of accumulation.

In that translation, in which the representational realm came to be supplanted by the material presence of property and the substantive generation of profit, class also registered as tragic loss, the balance sheet scarred by death itself. On January 31, 1989, Polydore St. Jean, a twenty-year veteran of the steel erection industry, tripped on the steel bridging of the Goodyear roof and sustained broken ribs, collarbone, and spine after plunging thirty feet to frozen ground. Hospitalized in Kingston, St. Jean died two and a half weeks later after a pulmonary embolism.

The Ontario Health and Safety Act requires workers labouring at a certain height to tie-off at all times, but St. Jean was engaged in work that was exempt from this regulation. The ironworker, a member of the United Steelworkers of America, was apparently not wearing a safety belt as he walked an eight-inch, steel I-beam carrying forty pounds of cross-bridging. "When we are working at places up high we have to be tied off with a safety belt," the injured man explained before his death. "But when you have to go more than forty feet to get bolts or something like that, you have to take it off." St. Jean became a statistic in the Construction Section of the Ontario Labour ministry's branch office: over the course of the late 1980s, 66 of the 177 provincial building trades' deaths registered with the ministry, or almost 40 per cent, were caused by falls.

The response to St. Jean's eventually fatal fall was revealing. Goodyear plant manager Kleckner could at first provide no details of the accident and claimed that the hospitalized worker had instructed the contractor, Nadrofsky Steel Erection of Brantford, not to release any information. Contacted by the press, St. Jean, suffering considerable pain, denied issuing any such directive and instead reported that Nadrofsky Steel had told him that they intended to make nothing about the fall public. Kleckner could offer no explanations for the crossed communications wires, but withdrew conveniently into the confines of family privacy. He said he had talked to two Kingston General Hospital officials who informed him that the St. Jean family was requesting that no information be released.

"Goodyear has built its reputation on integrity and we have an obligation to the family not to release any information regarding the accident," Kleckner said. Yet St. Jean himself talked to the press, as did his ex-wife Louise and his sister Darquise Sharron, who said her brother Polydore was "in shock" and could remember little about the serious fall. Later on his entire family attended an inquest into his death and was far from reluctant to reply to questions from journalists. It appeared that "the *people* people," these laid-back, down-to-earth guys with the proverbial gift of the gab, clammed up in certain situations.

Nothing could be got out of Jack Sinclaire, owner-president of Nadrofsky Steel. But at the coroner's inquest in May, Sinclaire opposed a suggested safety system composed of a set of horizontal cables that would form a guardrail throughout high-steel construction sites, allowing workers to tie-off wherever they had to be working. "I realize you can't put a price on life and limb, but the cost factor is undetermined as yet," said Sinclaire, who stressed that on small job sites the cable guardrail would be economically impractical. Both Sinclaire and Ontario Ministry of Labour investigator James Wilkinson seemed united in their views that costs prohibited the implementation of the cable system and that ironworkers were adamant that they would not "tie-off under those circumstances." But the inquest also heard testimony that the cable guardrails were in generalized use in Quebec, where use of the system was close to becoming mandatory under the law, and where a researcher with the Quebec health and safety board insisted that costs were minimal and implementation resulted in "a significant decline in fall-related deaths on sites using the system."

With this in mind, Coroner Benoit Bechard attacked the Ontario ministry and its waffling over mandatory safety measures in structural steel erection. "You're infuriating me," he exclaimed to Wilkinson. In turn Wilkinson responded to suggestions that the Ontario act be revised, removing the ambiguity around regulations concerning safety-belt use at a distance from specific work stations, with a cavalier acknowledgement that he would take the idea up with his superiors. "It's not your staff that need to be informed, it's your regulation that needs to be rewritten," Bechard said.

With thirty-nine deaths in the construction industry in Ontario in 1988, and following a lack of action on a previous coroner's jury recommendation surrounding the death of an Oshawa worker in 1986, Bechard had apparently had enough.[13] St. Jean, meanwhile, represented little more than a tragic occasion to pass the buck, which travelled from Goodyear to a Brantford contractor to a distant regulatory agency of the state.

None of this had much of an impact given the depressed eastern Ontario labour market, the declining possibilities of local farming, and the realities of working-class job conditions. By the time Goodyear's Phase One was nearing completion and its first 320 workers were scheduled to be hired, eastern Ontario was moving into the downward recessionary spiral of the late 1980s/early 1990s, which made Goodyear look exceedingly attractive to young job-seekers and older workers burned by the insecurities and injuries (hidden and overt) associated with dependency on the wage. Major regional employers such as Bombardier's Millhaven UTDC plant, Petco, and Celanese Canada issued layoff notices to five hundred workers in March 1989. Goodyear opened up possibilities for such displaced labour.

A thirty-nine-year-old machinist explained that he was in the process of being laid off from UTDC, while he had previously "helped to close" the Man Lepper plant in Napanee. "Work ... is very unpredictable," he noted, indicating also that his co-workers at UTDC were now quite disgruntled. To him the financial wherewithal of a multinational corporate giant suggested the kind of job continuity he needed.

A former NDSS student plugged into the local high-school-Goodyear connection held high hopes for the hiring: "They say they want Napanee high school graduates ... [and] I have a post-secondary education as well." For some, born into the rural chores of eastern Ontario farms, working in the tire industry seemed to offer an attractive change of pace. Describing himself as "just a poor farm boy," a six-foot, five-inch twenty-six-year-old complained: "I milk cows twice a day and I've done it for ten years and I'm getting sick of it. Milking cows is fun, but it's a lot of hard work. The pay's alright, but just the same, you like to advance." A young woman spoke for her husband, employed in a small local foundry: "What he's doing now in the summer must be 150 degrees, so anything would be better than that." Two Trenton labourers heard from friends who worked on the Goodyear construction site that job openings were available. They hoped "to get lucky."[14]

Those "fortunate" enough to land a job with Goodyear were almost certainly not hired for their diverse skills and mastery of technology, although background knowledge and experience were undoubtedly important. Goodyear recognizes no apprenticeship programs and has little interest in contributing to any institutionalized acknowledgement of trade skills. More central is "attitude." New workers at the Napanee division entered a highly controlled work environment. Like Goodyear's Lawton, Oklahoma, facility, the eastern Ontario plant was "under constant computer monitoring, from the raw materials receiving area to the finished products coming off the line." The interior of the factory — done in pastels of yellow and green with a yellowish tint to the lighting — is apparently spacious and spotlessly clean, lined with machines that do the cooking and cutting of tire production. Everything moves through the plant on conveyor belts, while stacking and storing are done by tall, elevator-type "vehicles" that resemble robots. By October 1990, four hundred computers were directing the technology, which appeared to an untrained eye as one vast machine with hundreds of components. In all of this the 320 "team members" (Goodyear apparently never uses the actual term "workers") were, according to a rare journalistic visitor allowed into the plant, "nearly invisible."

Workers in the industry do not find this setup surprising. They comment that the machinery literally surrounds labour, leaving tire-production workers very much out of the usual lines of sight. Responsible for a number of machines, each Goodyear operative monitors computers and keeps an eye on the performance of respective "machines." In continuous seven-day operation, twenty-four hours a day, Goodyear's weekly work rhythms are governed by twenty-one rotating "teams" or crews. Team members are expected to show up at the plant thirty minutes before their scheduled shift time to have an unpaid "team" conference, a coach's corner without the need for a coach. A consulting group hired by Goodyear eases workers and their families through the stress associated with this shift work.[15]

Approaching full-capacity production in the spring of 1993, Napanee's Goodyear plant was employing 550 people. With the company drawing its labour from the eastern Ontario counties of Lennox and Addington (39 per cent), Frontenac (26 per cent), Hastings (27 per cent), and Prince Edward, the bulk of the newly assembled employees were not even residing in Napanee. With an average age of thirty-one, few were recent NDSS graduates and many were obviously from non-union backgrounds, human material with a predilection to be adopted into and shaped by the Goodyear Corporate "Family."

Producing roughly fifteen thousand tires daily, the company's six million tires built over the course of 1990-93 supplied Goodyear service centres and Sears stores in the United States, but its major corporate customers were the auto manufacturers: Chrysler in Windsor and Bramalea, Ford in Oakville and Missouri, General Motors in Oshawa and St. Therese, Honda in Alliston, and Toyota in Cambridge. Most Canadian car and truck production, as well as two-thirds of the much larger U.S. automotive output, is within a day's shipping time, and a fleet of tractor-trailer trucks is usually parked close by the Napanee plant. Special orders have been commissioned around the world, with deliveries sent to Japan and Luxembourg.

Adaptable to future changes in market and production needs, the recently constructed factory is timeless, according to Kleckner. "This plant should be immortal," he told *The Financial Post*. Hailed by Akron headquarters as its premier production facility — cost-efficient, flexible, running on a "just-in-time" basis, and technologically sophisticated — Goodyear Napanee is championed as a showcase, the winner of corporate "Mark of Excellence" awards and kudos from the Industrial Designers Society of America.[16]

But as a showcase Goodyear Napanee is peculiarly reticent to expose itself to public scrutiny. What is in fact showcased in the local plant is, once again, the corporate ideology of familialism. Preparations for a "Team Appreciation Day" in spring 1992 highlighted both Goodyear's security fetish and its accent on attaining "global superiority" through productivity sustained by the ties of kinship, metaphorical and real, and its shop-floor equivalent, "team performance." The families of team members were to tour the plant in various slotted groups from noon until ten in the evening, first passing through several registration and security checks. They would see a promotional video and end their Goodyear visit at an informal buffet/reception where gifts were to be distributed. Team Appreciation Day preparations included the photographing of all team members' spouses and parents. According to *Tire Tracks*, the photos were taken for two reasons: "for security purposes" and so special commemorative identity badges could be given to "each visitor as a special memento of their time at Goodyear Napanee."

Kleckner explained that while Goodyear Napanee "has a high security environment with people only entering the plant who have a 'need to know,'" the families of team members did indeed qualify for admission to the facility. "We realize," he stressed, "that the quiet support of Team Members' families make our Team Members' efforts as great as they are.... Without them our performance would be significantly less." (The company noted, however, that "babysitting" would be unavailable.)

In seeing first-hand "a globally superior team in action," families of the Goodyear workers would appreciate "the new industrial environment" and witness how "the old dirty factory environment and autocratic management systems are things of the past." They would also appreciate that in future "troubled economic times," Goodyear Napanee was the family's best economic bet: "Our team is positioned to provide maximum job security in the global tire business for our Team Members."

Laying great stress on "the close knit team that deals directly with each other, has fun and knows the global challenge that exists," Kleckner linked issues of productivity and community, family and international competition, in a corporate adaptation of the pseudo-political "think global/act local" pop psychologizing of the 1980s. In the "one-to-one relationship" setting of tire output that was Goodyear Napanee, Kleckner promoted much-vaunted family values and needs as the foundation of "a special place with special people, producing special products in a special environment." He wanted team members to overcome "any hesitation" on the part of spouses or parents about coming to Team Appreciation Day.

"There will probably not be another event like this for several years," Kleckner suggested. "In all of my career," he said, "I cannot recall a time or more intense anticipation than the one coming up when we will be able to show our families what has been brought together."[17]

All of this fit well with the Goodyear corporate motto: "People Are

Carol Condé & Karl Beveridge in collaboration with C.E.W.C

■ **Re-imagining the team concept**

Our Most Important Asset."[18] Rooted in the almost-century old traditions of Litchfieldian industrial republicanism, this company philosophy ironically raised employed workers high on the page of the business ledgers, but in the process it nevertheless reduced them and their families to the status of a thing to be worked on and used as a means of proceeding with corporate development. Goodyear's team members, as assets, are different in degree but not in kind from other properties and resources. Like machines and land they can be appreciated or depreciated — as Etobicoke's workers learned the hard way — and even within the process of appreciation there is more than enough capitalist room for debasement and a distorted sense of value.

Team Appreciation Day was meant to showcase Goodyear Napanee to the narrowed extended family of direct producers that now mattered to company executives. If the July 1988 Friendship Festival placed Goodyear in the larger public eye, the 1992 Team Appreciation Day reflected a change in the corporation's concern about image. With the plant built and operative, with tires rolling off the line, Goodyear was no longer centrally motivated by the need to construct the widest possible support. Its concerted attempt to focus a favourable gaze could now constrict, marshalling and orchestrating the imagery of teamwork throughout the kinship circles of paid employees, rather than throughout the wider field of Napanee and eastern Ontario as a whole. This was possible for the company precisely because the primitive accumulation of hegemony was an accomplished fact by the late 1980s. Team appreciation days were simply the continuities in the costs of construction, a modest investment in building the human assets of tire production up to company specifications.

They were not, as such, centrally important in Goodyear's invasion of Napanee. That had already happened. "The rest," as NDSS student Karen Snowdon commented in 1988, "is history."[19]

Chapter Ten

The Contested Meanings of History

This notion — that events unfold in a way that produces a seemingly logical and inevitable set of future occurrences — recurs in the commentary on Goodyear's coming to Napanee. The engine of historical progression moves, partly by active human guidance to be sure, but once the initial track is seemingly laid the course is supposedly set.

Indeed, Goodyear Canada's official history recounts how its first Canadian plant, in Bowmanville, Ontario, received its initial large order for seventy tires from the McLaughlin Motor Car Company of Oshawa. Under the pressures of a three-day deadline, the company increased its staff, worked twenty-four-hour, three-shift days, and managed to deliver the goods on time. Enhancing Goodyear's reputation, this early success "launched the company on a course that would eventually establish [it] as the leader in the Canadian tire and rubber industry. The rest," concludes a seventy-five-year commemorative volume, "is history."[1]

Journalistic comment about Goodyear's final choice of Napanee stressed the conveniently videotaped student assembly as the final "cause" of corporate decision-making, which then proceeded in certain directions. "The rest is history — at least almost," concluded *Whig-Standard* reporters as Akron officials announced their guarded intentions and conditions for building a tire plant in Napanee in March 1988.[2] In such accounts, history is propelled forward by some meta-event, and then it just happens. And this happening does not necessarily require rethinking or interrogation.

A dual denigration of historical process underlies this seemingly commonsensical view of the relation of past, present, and future. First, origins, causality, importance, and meaning in the past are implicitly downplayed in their significance. "The rest is history" conjures up a sense of the past as irretrievably past, as what is done, as opposed to what needs doing, severing all kinds of relationships in and across time. Once set in motion, history is what does not matter any more. Second, this fixed viewpoint loses any sense of history as an ongoing and shifting set of outcomes of specific contending interests, as a struggle — however masked or innocuous — in which the coherence of the past, such as it is, emerges only momentarily out of particular contests among unequal parties, where victories and defeats are registered through the judicious wielding of blunt power and the more supple authority of consensual notions of legitimization. "The order of history emerges from the history of order," notes the conservative Eric Voegelin, while the Marxist historians Elizabeth Fox-Genovese and Eugene D. Genovese insist that history is about "who rides whom and how."[3]

With the history of power thus marginalized, it is not surprising that in the twentieth century there has been an unease with attempts to invest history with meaning. In the name of postmodernism and poststructuralism, current *fin de siècle* intellectual trends privilege a pervasive skepticism concerning history. Both in terms of history as a written discipline, aiming to uncover the meanings of the past, and as a lived experience within which people find themselves both subjectively influential and objectively influenced, history is now scrutinized with intense doubt.

As Pauline Marie Rosenau comments, "For skeptical post-modernists, history, if it exists at all, is a humble discipline, dependent on the present, without any integrity of its own." Postmodernism posits an almost disembodied and fragmented contemporaneity as the site of history as a *happening*, a "series of perpetual presents." Analytic thought can be poststructuralist, suggests Fredric Jameson, only as it liberates itself from the chains of various forms of "*historical* thinking."[4]

Whatever the complex meanings of poststructuralism or postmodernism and the often vehement extent to which they assault the significance of the past, suspicions about antagonisms towards history are far from strikingly new. Modernist philosophy, literature, and popular culture are stained with the blood of history spilled in a series of sharp, dismissive blows. To be sure, there is a difference between the postmodernist rejection of history and modernist commentary, which contains a persistent anti-historicism. For Nietzsche (1882) history was "belief in falsehood," a "storage costume where all the falsehoods are kept." In James Joyce's *Ulysses* (1922) history was "a nightmare" from which it is necessary to awake. Henry Ford (1916) thought history "more or less bunk."[5] But these assessments *of* history differentiate themselves from postmodern challenges *to* its possibility precisely to the extent that they acknowledge that history, negatively conceived, is about hurt, about images of (apparently important) illusion, about denials that (by implication) have to be made for interested reasons, for the preservation of power and the making of profit. They stand somewhat in contrast, in Jameson's words, to "the postmodern," which "invites us to indulge a somber mockery of historicity in general, wherein the effort at self-consciousness with which our own situation somehow completes the act of historical understanding, repeats itself drearily as in the worst kinds of dreams and juxtaposes, to its own pertinent philosophical repudiation of the very concept of self-consciousness, a grotesque carnival of the latter's various replays."[6]

This is not unrelated to the commonplace refusals of "the rest is history" *or* the narrative of Goodyear's invasion of Napanee. For central to an understanding of the meaning of the Akron multinational's coming to eastern Ontario is an appreciation of the extent to which Goodyear actually *made* history (and almost as it pleased).[7] This history was a project of conscious construction, distortion, and manipulation that layered the past in meanings that have and will continue to have meanings in the present and the future. The rest was not *just* history; the rest was built on and out of a past that was presented as a kind of cultural text.

That cultural text preceded and prepared the way for economic relations of appropriation and accumulation that were themselves the material foundation and purpose behind Goodyear's conquest of the backcountry. The men from Akron care for culture, representation, and image — let me be blunt in saying — only in so much as these efforts pay. From the days of Litchfield's industrial republicanism they have found that dividends from these sources can indeed be handsome. If capital is to reproduce itself, and imperialistically conquer new zones of seeming marginality, culture is a useful conduit, and what is created for the public eye matters.

Reading this culture and this constructed vision, as Jameson reads the literary canon, is thus a project governed by the imperative of dialectical thought, "Always historicize!" We must apprehend the narrative of Goodyear's invasion of Napanee through "sedimented layers" that reach above and beyond locale, "grasped as vital episodes in a single vast unfinished plot." Jameson argues that "detecting the traces of that uninterrupted narrative" can restore "to the surface of the text the

repressed and buried reality" of a "fundamental history" of class relations. In the process cultural artifacts and undertakings are unmasked
as socially symbolic acts, the site of "the political unconscious."[8] Making
that undertaking of political economy conscious, exposing its obscure
and at times invisible meanings to public view, rather than allowing
them to remain as part of the routinely ignored "rest" that is merely a
happened history, is a necessary beginning in the act of resistance.

Carole Condé & Karl Beveridge in collaboration with the C.E.W.C.

■ Past, present, future: The linked meanings that do not die

Indeed, chipping away at the constructed primitive accumulation of hegemony that is now Goodyear's historic legacy in the Napanee region commences with a scrutiny of just how the corporate multinational *made* that history. For the Akron tire firm created this history in ways that did indeed hurt some even as it seductively entrapped others. Etobicoke's aged, unionized workers were the first casualties in the making of Goodyear's Napanee. Their jobs lost, their pensions and severance benefits the object of considerable dispute, their identities eroded, the tire builders and other workers, many of whose families go back in the Goodyear New Toronto facility for decades, knew well that "the rest is history" did not exactly speak to the traumas of their own experience. This was not, however, a message that was destined to sell in the job-starved small eastern Ontario town of Napanee.

To deflect this hurt in the historical process, Goodyear and its Napanee allies mobilized and embellished the positive (and positively) *local* attractions of Napanee, most especially its youth at the local secondary school. There was no overt conspiracy in this unfolding history, only a kind of unquestioned consensual framework. The logic of events and of their making was widely and implicitly understood even to the point of being unchallengeable. As Goodyear executives championed the initiative and spirit of the students, who had been prodded to action by educational administrators and counsellors, the mythology of the December 1987 NDSS Student Council assembly was constructed. This became the meta-event of historical decision-making, in which "the rest" (before *and* after) was indeed little more than history.

Journalists picked up on the status of the student assembly and regularly incorporated its importance into their accounts, without talking to Student Council president Mark Arsenault or other council members. The result was that the student assembly became inscribed in the printed descriptive texts of Goodyear's coming to Napanee as a kind of turning point. This, in conjunction with the supposed failure of the "community" to attract the company being turned into success at the eleventh hour, also helped enshrine the assembly in the folk memory of the Goodyear-Napanee relation. Stripped of its content, which almost no one actually bothers to try to know or question, the student assembly looms larger than actual life in the making of Goodyear's presence in Napanee.

Yet the much-mentioned video of the Student Council assembly provides a striking testament to the assembly's thoroughly mundane content and brief duration. Arsenault's speech is less than three minutes long and there are no other student talks or questions from the audience; the most emphatic statement comes from the school principal, Rod Hughes. The students themselves are not wildly enthusiastic and pro-company: they are sitting and waiting on the gym floor; their clapping is somewhat perfunctory and lackadaisical; they make their way out of the assembly and file past the video equipment with just the kind of divergent indifference you would expect from a youthful crowd with other things on its varied and wandering mind.

These students do not look like the kind of human material that will draw the corporate big money and be championed in the local and national business press, that will, five years later, be the subject of a Canadian Broadcasting Corporation *Venture* television program. They appear to be concerned with matters that have very little to do with Goodyear coming to Napanee: the day's classes and the abbreviated first period of the interrupted school morning; the cliques and friendships that have defined their being for months, maybe years; the presentation of themselves to the camera in the many possible guises of "cool." But then students were not really the reason Goodyear chose Napanee; that decision was made for other more directly economic reasons. To think that this video actually "won" Goodyear's Akron executives to Napanee is, upon viewing the actual document, ludicrous. The student assembly is now routinely cited as *the* central event propelling Goodyear and Napanee into a situation in which "the rest is [merely] history" because in this active *making* of history specific ends were nicely served: the visible hurt of Etobicoke was blocked out in congratulatory bows to student enthusiasm; education as the cultivation of attitude and job initiative was confirmed; and the promise of entrepreneurial potential played nowhere as positively as in a community made rightly proud of its youth.[9]

For its part, when addressing other audiences more in tune with the bigger pictures of accumulation on a world scale and the Akron company's quest for market dominance, Goodyear promoted a different appreciation of what was at issue in its choice of Napanee. At shareholders' meetings and in Akron itself, Goodyear chairman Robert E. Mercer stressed that Napanee was ideally located to be the company's next site because of the Canadian state's domestic-content rules, government aid, and geographic proximity to U.S. producers and the growing

Canadian automobile sector, estimated to dominate 75 per cent of all future growth in the industry in North America. Students did not merit a mention.[10] Goodyear obviously lived by attending to its self-identification, as if what you have done depends on whom you are talking to: history is meant to be *made*.

From the vantage point of hindsight this is all too apparent even in terms of Goodyear's visual representation of the plant-to-be. Goodyear presented artist sketches of the proposed facility to the regional audience at an April 1988 open house, and the pictures were duly reproduced in area newspapers. With Akron managers of plant public relations in attendance, Goodyear stressed that the new tire factory would "fit in with and become an asset to the community." Proposing an "attractive" building that would blend well with "its natural surroundings," company officials promised "landscaping, about three spring-fed ponds, and there could be a golf course, tennis courts, and a recreation centre." The artistic presentation of the future factory makes the facility look almost resort-like.

Deceptively congenial, the world's most modern radial tire plant was to be sleek and unobtrusive, a productive adornment to a natural habitat enhanced by the sculpting hand of caring human construction. This *is* a pretty picture. Captivated by the conscious aesthetics of company presentation, most comment on the *drawing* of the factory took Goodyear at its artistic word and further deepened a conception of the future tire plant that played into Akron's obvious attempt to beautify the unbuilt. "Picture a very narrow rectangular structure in the midst of

■ **Artist sketch of proposed Goodyear plant, 1988**

a landscaped park, boasting no less than three spring-fed ponds, and perhaps a tennis court or two," commented *The Whig-Standard*, in what seemed a pitch for a playground rather than a workplace. "Very stream-lined," was the more subdued response of one resident.[11]

Pictures certainly can be worth thousands of words. So can before and after shots. But in the case of Goodyear the before/after compar-isons are disappointing: the promotional price of the representations and rhetoric of 1988 paid in the letdown of the realization that great expectations have not turned into actualities.

While the Goodyear plant is no doubt modern and clean, stream-lined compared to the sooty smokestack factories of earlier times, it bears only the most formal resemblance to the artistic presentations of 1988. There are no tennis courts and golf courses; the spring-fed ponds are, for much of the year, murky mud-holes; and the landscaping so far has been dominated by the unkempt scrub bush and displaced boulders that remain after a massive material intervention into the local ecology. Contrasting with the "air-brushed" aesthetics of an artist's drawing is the blunt sight of a seemingly endless edifice of corrugated steel, largely windowless, secured at all points by gates, guards, and fences, bounded by huge industrial cylinders, enmeshed in the dangers of high voltage wiring. Whatever this may be in the comparative terms of North America workplaces, it is not parkland.

Goodyear's presentation, then, exceeded, by a long shot, what it delivered. The final picture proves anything but pretty. The rest is not just history: it is a reminder that history is about outcomes that are not necessarily projected and promised.

This truism presents some space for hope. Goodyear has made history in the eastern Ontario region largely because it has had a free hand in constructing that history, and in enshrining it in myth. The outcomes *have* been those that capital in general, and a specific firm in particular, find to their liking. There have been many in the Napanee "community"

Neil Ward

■ Goodyear at a glance

Nicholas Rogers

■ Streamlined and bleak

Neil Ward

■ As close as you get

who have embraced Goodyear's invasion, promoted it, and profited as it ran its course. But there are also those who now dissent, however quietly and ineffectively.

To be sure, the displaced Goodyear workers in Etobicoke are largely forgotten; but local NDSS graduates — if the ones I talked to are at all typical — have largely embraced the understandable cynicism of those who were paid for their supposedly pivotal support with a blank cheque that has ended bouncing up in their still-jobless faces. Established regional trades workers have for the most part found Goodyear uninterested in their skills and experience. The company has instead opted for more pliant workers with no apprenticeship training or unionized pasts. Labour is only wanted at Goodyear if it can be moulded to the corporate project.

Many workers refuse to enter into such blatantly one-sided work relations, even in today's climate of recession and job scarcity. It is not difficult to find, scattered across the eastern Ontario landscape, electricians, tool-and-die makers, machinists, and others who, after being interviewed for hours and getting to the second and third stages of Goodyear's "screening" of job applicants, have thrown in the economistic towel. Whatever the pay, they tell you, the cost in dignity and self-worth is just too high. These are not the labourers quoted in the journalistic stories of thousands lining up at the local high school, hoping for a one-in-twenty shot at getting hired. But they will tell you their stories as they tend to their lawns, pull themselves out from under the hoods of their trucks, drop their lines into Lake Ontario when the Walleye season opens in May, or sit on local barstools. They are the voices that won't be heard inside fortress Goodyear.

As of now that fortress is partially protected by the moat of a history that Goodyear both created and interpreted, and that few care to traverse with the challenge of an alternative assessment. Complacent in its successful making of history, Goodyear has retreated into its productive purpose. Content to be but one of many corporate team players in the sponsorship of regional events, the company no longer has a need to be highly visible. It has recently even taken down its prominent highway billboard. Its ideological project has been refocused, turned inward on the plant and its workforce, rather than directed to external constituencies in the Napanee region as it was in the preconstruction period of the late 1980s.

Metaphors of family ties, once used to link Goodyear and the Napanee region, now enclose workers, managers, and the Akron multinational in a circle of productivist kinship. Output and teamwork are the new, narrower subject of promotion, extolled in the plant paper, *Tire Tracks*, broadcast over the Goodyear radio channel, CMWC 93.3 FM, twenty-four hours daily, and drummed into the selective workforce assembled with painstaking care by Akron-trained personnel managers.

Apparently highly successful, Goodyear's team approach to production is in fact something of a self-fulfilling prophecy. Workers get jobs with Napanee's largest employer only if they are willing to subordinate both their individuality and their collectivity to the corporation's understanding of the priorities of the workplace. Once the pact has been made with that particular devil, the rest, seemingly, is again little more than history happening: crews are formed; workplace friendships are consolidated; tires are produced; paycheques are cashed.[12] History becomes nothing more than an endless, repetitive cycle of Goodyear-centred activity, routinized and regularized as life itself, broken only by times of replenishment with family, friends, and the outdoors.

But the team concept — even unencumbered by unionism as it is at Goodyear's Napanee plant — carries with it a set of internal inconsistencies and contradictions, most of them related to the obscured history of unequal class relations.[13] To grasp that history is to appreciate that an Etobicoke worker's pain and loss are no less significant than a Napanee youth's hopeful sense of possibility. Being attentive to that history means understanding that on the Goodyear team some players are more equal than others: Robert Mercer's 1988 salary and bonus options totalled almost $1.3 million U.S. dollars, placing him in a significantly different income category than a $17-an-hour tire builder; Mercer's stake in the company, with over ten thousand Goodyear Tire and Rubber shares tucked away in his portfolio, hardly compares to that of a mail-room employee.[14]

This same history shows that over time, whatever the aspirations and illusions of a workforce cultivated to think along the lines of the corporate agenda, work and its discontents do eventually expose some of capitalism's many Achilles heels, however quickly entrepreneurial socks are darned. Team players learn the rules of capitalism's game, and when and how they can be broken by some but not by others. These lessons come episodically and unevenly, to be sure, but persistently nonetheless, as they did in Akron's Wobbly-led strike of 1913, in the upsurge of the CIO in Ohio in the mid-1930s and in Ontario in the 1940s, as well as in the hard fall of Etobicoke's unionists in 1986-87.

Napanee's Goodyear team is new in many senses of the word. Its acknowledgement of this history is now weak and purposely directed to appreciate one side only of the past. But over time it, too, will gain a sense of the contested meaning of history, of how history conditions the present and the future. When it does it will gain new insights, indeed new ways of seeing. Everything will look different, including how Goodyear's brand of capitalism came to the backcountry of eastern Ontario in the late 1980s. At that point of possibility the rest will not be history; the rest will remake history.

■ Looking at class

NEW PLANT MANAGER AT GOODYEAR NAPANEE

A new plant manager will be taking over at Goodyear Napanee on July 1, 1993. Mr. Tom Jindra arrives after serving as Goodyear's vice president of production at the plant in Santiago, Chile.

Bill Vankoughnet, M.P. joins with all area residents in welcoming Mr. Jindra and his wife Diane to the area, and extending best wishes for the future to outgoing plant manager K.B. Kleckner who is to become plant manager of Goodyear's facility in Lawton, Oklahoma.

Bill Vankoughnet, M.P. met with Mr. Kleckner (left) and Mr. Jindra (centre) recently at Goodyear Napanee.

Bill Vankoughnet, *Report from Parliament*, July 1993

■ Postscript: The Personal/Personnel is political

Notes

Abbreviations

AVS, GF: "Goodyear File," compiled by Adrian Van Asseldonk, Manager, Canada Employment and Immigration, Napanee.

DBF: David Birrell Files, United Rubber, Cork, Linoleum, and Plastic Workers of America, Local 232, Etobicoke, Ont.

NDSS: Napanee District Secondary School.

VF, NPL: Napanee History Vertical File, Napanee Public Library.

1. A Billboard in My Backyard

1. Jimmy Reed, "Bright Lights, Big City," and "Big Boss Man," Chameleon Records, 1988 VeeJay Hall of Fame Series.

2. Maurice O'Reilly, *The Goodyear Story* (Elmsford, N.Y.: Benjamin, 1983), pp.181-82.

3. "Provinces Stalled on Tire Disposal," *The Globe and Mail*, Jan. 2, 1993.

4. Paulette Peirol, "Site Sketches Show Streamlined Plant," *The Whig-Standard* (Kingston), April 15, 1988. Shelley Aylesworth-Spink, Communications Specialist for Goodyear in Napanee, attributed the concern with security to the company fear of industrial espionage. She claimed other Canadian tire manufacturers had been engaged in efforts to spy on the new technology in the plant and responded to my request to see the inside of Goodyear operations with an apologetic, but unambiguously firm, dismissal of such a tour. Perhaps this would be possible in five years, she indicated, but certainly not now. Phone conversation with Shelley Aylesworth-Spink, Feb. 22, 1993. Press coverage of an early Goodyear open house at Selby noted, "Residents yesterday didn't seem to mind Goodyear's corporate policy of confidentiality—which company executives say will be just as strict once the plant opens." See "If This Means Jobs, I'm on Your Side," *The Whig-Standard*, April 15, 1988.

5. Consider the passages on sexuality, gender, animality, and industrialism in Antonio Gramsci, *Selections from the Prison Notebooks* (New York: International, 1971), pp.294-301.

2. Concepts and Context: Democratic Aesthetics and the Imagery of Incorporation

1. The literature here is immense. The classic collection of articles on the transition from feudalism to capitalism is Rodney Hilton et al., *The Transition from Feudalism to Capitalism* (London: New Left Books, 1976), but the debate around this question has since shifted to new ground. See, for instance, T.H. Aston and C.H.E. Philpin, eds., *The Brenner Debate: Agrarian Class Structure and Economic Development in Pre-Industrial Europe* (Cambridge: Cambridge University Press, 1985). On protoindustrialization, the initial statement was Franklin Mendels, "Proto-industrialization: The First Phase of the Industrializing Process," *Journal of Economic History*, 32 (1972), pp.241-61. For demography, Wally Seccombe, *A Millennium of Family Change: Feudalism to Capitalism in Northwestern Europe* (London: Verso, 1992) is unsurpassed in its insights and breadth. For the United States and Canada, note, as well, Steven Hahn and Jonathan Prude, eds., *The Countryside in the Age of Capitalist Transformation* (Chapel Hill: University of North Carolina Press, 1985); Michael Merrill, "'Cash Is Good To Eat': Self-Sufficiency and Exchange in the Rural Economy of the United States," *Radical History Review*, 3 (1977), pp.42-71; Bryan D. Palmer, "Town, Port, and Country: Speculations on the Capitalist Transformation of Canada," *Acadiensis*, 12 (1983), pp.131-39; and the essays in Danny Samson, ed., *Contested Countryside: Rural Workers and Modern Society in Atlantic Canada, 1800-1950* (Fredericton, N.B.: Acadiensis Press, 1994).

2. Background texts include E.P. Thompson, *Customs in Common* (London: Merlin Press, 1991); and Raymond Williams, *The Country and the City* (London: Chatto and Windus, 1973).

3. Marxist geographers have offered considerable comment on corporate and spatial restructuring. See Doreen Massey, *Spatial Divisions of Labour: Social Structures and the Geography of Production* (London: Macmillan, 1984); Allen J. Scott and Michael Storper, eds., *Production, Work, Territory: The Geographical Anatomy of Industrial Capitalism* (Boston: Allen & Unwin, 1986); and David Harvey, *The Condition of Postmodernity: An Enquiry into the Origins of Cultural Change* (Oxford: Basil Blackwell, 1989). While valuable, this work perhaps understates the extent to which geographic shifts in industrial location are an old story. Note the discussion of the tire industry in John Dean Gaffey, *The Productivity of Labor in the Rubber Tire Manufacturing Industry* (New York: Columbia University Press, 1940), pp.149-75 and the general points in Andrew Sayer and Richard Walker, *The New Social Economy: Reworking the Division of Labor* (Cambridge, Mass.: Blackwell, 1992).

   A useful overview of the literature on flexibility is Martha MacDonald, "Post-Fordism and the Flexibility Debate," *Studies in Political Economy*, 36 (1991), pp.177-201. See, as well, E. Schoenburger, "From Fordism to Flexible Accumulation: Technology, Competitive Strategies, and Internal Location," *Environment and Planning D: Society and Space*, 6 (1988), pp.245-62; Sayer and Walker, *New Social Economy*; and Michael H. Best, *The New Competition: Institutions of Industrial Restructuring* (Oxford: Basil Blackwell, 1990).

   On governments and industrial policy, see Daniel Drache and Meric

Gertler, eds., *The New Era of Global Competition: State Policy and Market Power* (Montreal and Kingston: McGill-Queen's University Press, 1991); and Paul Hirst and Jonathan Zeitlin, eds., *Reversing Industrial Decline? Industrial Structure and Policy in Britain and Her Competitors* (New York: St. Martin's Press, 1989).

4. Karl Marx and Frederick Engels, "Manifesto of the Communist Party," in Marx and Engels, *Selected Works* (Moscow: Progress Books, 1968), p.38. Also, Marshall Berman, *All That Is Solid Melts into Air: The Experience of Modernity* (New York: Simon and Schuster, 1982).

5. On Fordism and labour, see Mike Davis, *Prisoners of the American Dream: Politics and Economy in the History of the US Working Class* (London: Verso, 1986); Bob Russell, *Back to Work? Labour, State, and Industrial Relations in Canada* (Toronto: Nelson, 1990); Bryan D. Palmer, *Working-Class Experience: Rethinking the History of Canadian Labour, 1800-1991*, 2nd ed. (Toronto: McClelland and Stewart, 1992).

6. Gordon L. Clark, *Unions and Communities Under Seige: American Communities and the Crisis of Organized Labor* (New York: Cambridge University Press, 1989), p.xi.

7. Herbert Marcuse, *One-Dimensional Man: Studies in the Ideology of Advanced Industrial Society* (Boston: Beacon Press, 1964), p.65. I use the term "manufacturing of consent" not in the Chomskyian sense of the limiting role of the modern bourgeois media, but in terms of corporate capital's capacity to create a climate of community compliance when jobs are at stake. For a brief outline of this process, see Steve Fox, "Albuquerque and GTE Lenkurt Recruit Each Other," in Fox, *Toxic Work: Women Workers at GTE Lenkurt* (Philadelphia: Temple University Press, 1991), pp.30-34.

8. Richard Rorty, *Philosophy and the Mirror of Nature* (Princeton, N.J.: Princeton University Press, 1979); Michel Foucault, *Discipline and Punish: The Birth of the Prison* (New York: Pantheon, 1977); Guy Debord, *Comments on the Society of the Spectacle* (London: Verso, 1990); Martin Jay, "Scopic Regimes of Modernity," in Jay, *Force Fields: Between Intellectual History and Cultural Critique* (New York: Routledge, 1993), pp.114-15.

9. Neil Evernden, *The Natural Alien: Humankind and Environment* (Toronto: University of Toronto Press, 1985), quoted in Alexander Wilson, *The Culture of Nature: North American Landscape from Disney to the Exxon Valdez* (Toronto: Between the Lines, 1991), p.122; Jacqueline Rose, *Sexuality in the Field of Vision* (London: Verso, 1986), pp.232-33.

10. I thus situate myself ambivalently in relation to other works that address "seeing." See, for instance, John Berger et al., *Ways of Seeing* (Harmondsworth, England: Penguin, 1972); Susan Buck-Morss, *The Dialectics of Seeing: Walter Benjamin and the Arcades Project* (Cambridge, Mass.: MIT Press, 1989). For critical appraisals of Berger, see Fred Inglis, *Radical Earnestness: English Social Theory, 1880-1980* (Oxford: Martin Robertson, 1982), pp.186-92; Harvey Kaye, "John Berger and the Question of History," in Kaye, *The Education of Desire: Marxists and the Writing of History* (New York: Routledge, 1992), pp.145-61. Note, as well, the useful discussions of place, space, and politics in Michael Keith and Steve Pile, eds., *Place and the Politics of Identity* (London and New York: Routledge, 1993), especially David Harvey, "Class Relations, Social Justice and the Politics of Difference," pp.41-66.

3. "Pre-History": Company and "Community"

1. *A note on currency*: where dollar figures are cited they are in U.S. or Canadian dollars, according to the obvious context. For instance, when I refer to Sir James Goldsmith receiving $620 million to stop his takeover bid of Goodyear, this is in U.S. dollars, while land prices and wage rates in Napanee are in Canadian dollars.

2. See Ralph F. Wolf, *India Rubber Man: The Story of Charles Goodyear* (Caldwell, Ida.: Caxton Printers, 1939). For the legal wranglings within the budding tire industry, seen from another corporation's vantage point, see Alfred Lief, *The Firestone Story: A History of the Firestone Tire and Rubber Company* (New York: McGraw-Hill, 1951), pp.108-10. Goodyear's place in the patent and technical evolution of the rubber industry is touched on in P. Schidrowitz and T.R. Dawson, eds., *History of the Rubber Industry* (Cambridge: W. Heffer & Sons, 1952).

    For the history of Goodyear, see Hugh Allen, *The House of Goodyear: Fifty Years of Men and Industry* (Cleveland: Corday & Gross, 1949); and O'Reilly, *Goodyear Story*. Unless otherwise noted, all figures relating to the company and its early history come from these sources.

3. For Goodyear's opportune relationship to new economic developments, see Paul W. Litchfield, *Industrial Voyage: My Life as an Industrial Lieutenant* (New York: Doubleday, 1954), pp.98-134. On the second industrial revolution in Canada a useful introduction is Craig Heron, "The Second Industrial Revolution in Canada, 1890-1930," in Deian R. Hopkin and Gregory S. Kealey, eds., *Class, Community and the Labour Movement: Wales and Canada, 1850-1930* (St. John's, Nfld.: Canadian Committee on Labour History, 1989), pp.48-66.

4. The standard corporate histories previously cited convey much of this information, but note as well John Dean Gaffey, *The Productivity of Labor in the Rubber Tire Manufacturing Industry* (New York: Columbia University Press, 1940).

5. Figures on Goodyear Canada come from Bill Reid, "Goodyear: A Big Wheel in Business," *The Whig Standard*, March 26, 1988. The Akron-based parent company claimed in 1988 to be producing five hundred thousand tires daily, generating an annual $10 billion. The number of plants and their employees had dropped from the early 1980s under the impetus of rationalization (ninety-four factories and 114,000 workers), but Goodyear had expanded to more countries, thirty-nine, including Japan and Greece. See Maxine Hagerman, "Could Be a Goodyear for Area!" *Napanee Beaver*, March 30, 1988. On Goodyear Canada, wartime production, and the post-World War II expansion, see *Goodyear Canada Inc.: The First 75 Years* (Toronto: Goodyear, 1985), quote from p.55.

6. See Litchfield, *Industrial Voyage*, p.92; O'Reilly, *Goodyear Story*, pp.134-35. The varsity basketball program was discontinued in 1970 at the height of a strike by the United Rubber Workers of America. Given the centrality of sport at Goodyear it is perhaps not surprising that a sit-down strike in Akron supposedly grew out of a dispute on a baseball diamond. Players from opposing factory

teams refused to play because the umpire was not a union man. They apparently simply sat down and demanded his replacement. See Jeremy Brecher, *Strike!* (San Francisco: Straight Arrow Books, 1972), pp.180-81, citing Louis Adamic, *My America, 1928-1938* (New York: Harper and Brothers, 1938), p.405.

7. See, for instance, Daniel Nelson, *Managers and Workers: Origins of the New Factory System in the United States, 1880-1920* (Madison: University of Wisconsin Press, 1975), pp.117, 145, 152; O'Reilly, *Goodyear Story*, pp.31-32, 56; Allen, *House of Goodyear*, pp.165-200; Lief, *Firestone Story*, p.101; Joseph A. McCartin, "'An American Feeling': Workers, Managers, and the Struggle over Industrial Democracy in the World War I Era," in Nelson Lichtenstein and Howell John Harris, eds., *Industrial Democracy in America: The Ambiguous Promise* (Cambridge: Cambridge University Press and Woodrow Wilson Centre Press, 1993), pp.84-85. For Canada, see *Goodyear Canada Inc.: The First 75 Years*, pp.42-43.

8. Litchfield, *Industrial Voyage*, pp.169-170.

9. Paul W. Litchfield, *The Industrial Republic: A Study in Industrial Economics* (Boston and New York: Houghton Mifflin, 1920), esp. pp.6-8. Also, Litchfield, *Industrial Voyage*, pp.130-33.

10. Litchfield, *Industrial Voyage*, pp.131-32. On the Akron strike, see also Lief, *Firestone Story*, pp.66-69; and Melvyn Dubofsky, *We Shall Be All: A History of the Industrial Workers of the World* (Chicago: Quadrangle, 1969), pp.286-87, which, counter to Litchfield, notes, "The strikers demanded not revolution but bread." For an immigrant worker's recollection of the Akron strike, see Stewart Bird, Dan Georgakas, Deborah Shaffer, eds., *Solidarity Forever: An Oral History of the IWW* (Chicago: Lakeview Press, 1985), pp.78-80, 88.

11. The relationship of labour conflict and the 1913 strike to the creation of the Flying Squadron is, interestingly, commented on explicitly in the first edition of Hugh Allen's company history, but in the revised 1949 edition the connection between the squadron and class conflict is less direct. See Hugh Allen, *The House of Goodyear* (Akron, Ohio: Superior Printing, 1936), esp. p.194; Allen, *House of Goodyear* (1949), p.188. My references throughout are to the 1949 edition unless otherwise noted.

12. For a general statement, see Robert W. Dunn, *The Americanization of Labor: The Employers' Offensive Against Trade Unions* (New York: International, 1927). When war broke out in 1914 Litchfield ruled that all employees must become U.S. citizens and learn to speak English, and this was the context in which Americanization classes were initiated, teachers hired, and the small immigrant workforce at Goodyear "trained" in the requisites of citizenship. See Allen, *House of Goodyear*, p.187. On the ethnic make-up of the rubberworker city of Akron—dominantly southern-born whites from West Virginia, Tennessee, and Alabama, but with a smattering (less than 10 per cent of the total population in 1939, but once supposedly as high as 20 per cent) of foreign-born immigrants—see Ruth McKenney, *Industrial Valley* (New York: Harcourt Brace and Company, 1939), and Gaffey, *Productivity of Labor*, pp.64-67.

13. Litchfield address quoted in O'Reilly, *Goodyear Story*, p.46; *Work of the Labor Division* quoted in Harold S. Roberts, *The Rubber Workers: Labor Organization*

and Collective Bargaining in the Rubber Industry (New York: Harper and Brothers, 1944), p.199. One dimension of Goodyear's "human" approach was its targeting of specific disadvantaged work groups and integrating them into its productive process. During World War I, for instance, a "colony" of deaf mutes, known as the "Silents," was employed at Goodyear. Allen, *House of Goodyear*, p.191, notes about these several hundred workers: "They worked harder than the average, feeling the necessity to make up for their handicap; they did not talk at work, since they would have to stop work in order to do so.... The great silence which surround the 'silents' helped them to concentrate, so that they learned the multitude of factory operations faster than other men." Twenty years later, during World War II, the company responded to labour shortages by hiring dwarfs, midgets, and the blind, who proved particularly useful, according to a company history, in accomplishing tasks that larger and sighted workers either could not do or would find exceedingly tedious. See O'Reilly, *Goodyear Story*, p.91.

14. See Litchfield, *Industrial Voyage*, pp.183-87, and *Industrial Republic*, pp.79-95. Goodyear may nevertheless have employed spies to keep an eye on possible union activity. See Roberts, *Rubber Workers*, p.196; Robert W. Dunn, *Spying on Workers* (New York: International Pamphlets, 1933), p.17.

15. This discussion draws on Roberts, *Rubber Workers*, pp.192-254; and Brecher, *Strike!*, pp.177-186. For colourful daily reports, see McKenney, *Industrial Valley*, which quotes Litchfield on pp.327-28.

16. Litchfield, *Industrial Voyage*, pp.257-61.

17. McKenney, *Industrial Valley*, p.224.

18. For a view of art and work, see Carole Condé and Karl Beveridge, *First Contract: Women and the Fight to Unionize* (Toronto: Between the Lines, 1986), pp.12-18. I have drawn on four of Condé's and Beveridge's artistic productions, all of which originally appeared in Condé and Beveridge, *Class Work* (Toronto: Communications Workers of Canada, 1990).

19. On the early history of Napanee, see Frank B. Edwards, *The Smiling Wilderness: An Illustrated History of Lennox and Addington County* (Camden East, Ont.: Camden House Publishing, 1984), pp.100-21; Jennifer Bunting, "An Upper Canadian Merchant, 1833: John Benson of Napanee," M.A. thesis, Queen's University, 1991, esp. pp.12-25; Walter S. Herrington, *History of the County of Lennox and Addington* (Toronto: Macmillan, 1913), pp.17-53, 73-96, 208-55; Brochure Committee of the Lennox and Addington Historical Society, *Historical Glimpses of Lennox and Addington County* (Napanee: Lennox and Addington County Council, 1964), pp.54-63; Maude Benson, "Napanee, The Pioneer Flour Town," clipping in VF, NPL.

20. "Industrial Napanee Today," in *Historical Glimpses of Lennox and Addington County*, pp.173-81. Population figures are from Edwards, *Smiling Wilderness*, p.117; *Industrial Data Manual for the Town of Napanee and Immediate Area* (Napanee: Napanee Industrial Committee, 1966), VF, NPL; Paulette Peirol, "Honda Town Helps Napanee Plan for Goodyear," *The Whig-Standard*, June 4, 1988.

21. "Business Men," *Napanee Standard*, 1864 facsimile, prepared by Lennox and Addington Historical Society, VF, NPL.

22. Quoted in Gregory S. Kealey and Bryan D. Palmer, *Dreaming of What Might Be: The Knights of Labor in Ontario, 1880-1900* (Toronto: New Hogtown Press, 1987), p.300.

23. *Industrial Data Manual for the Town of Napanee*, VF, NPL.

24. *The Whig-Standard*, May 19, 1992; "Goodyear Said Planning Plant To Employ 800 in Eastern Ontario," *The Toronto Star*, undated; John Geddes, "The Making of the Big Time in a Small Town," *The Financial Post*, May 30, 1988; all AVS, GF. Also, information from Adrian Van Asseldonk, telephone conversation, Feb. 22, 1993. Ontario industry minister Monte Kwinter referred to the Goodyear plant coming to Napanee as "a tremendous economic boost" for "chronically depressed eastern Ontario." See *The Whig-Standard*, March 24, 1988.

25. H.W. Webster, letter to the editor, *The Whig-Standard*, April 16, 1988; "Job-starved Napanee Tipped as Goodyear Site," *The Toronto Star*, March 25, 1988.

4. "Cloak and Dagger" Beginnings: The Price of Property

1. Geddes, "Making of the Big Time in a Small Town"; Paulette Peirol, "Mystery Firm Seeks Industrial Rezoning," *The Whig-Standard*, March 22, 1988; Reid, "Goodyear: A Big Wheel in Business."

2. Dunnery Best, "Hot Goodyear Canada Leaves Shareholders Cold," *Financial Times of Canada*, April 20-26, 1992, in AVS, GF. This section also draws on Gordon Pitts, "A Tale of Two Ontario Companies," *The Financial Post*, July 16, 1990; Paulette Peirol, "MPP: If I Was Napanee Mayor I'd Want Some Guarantees," *The Whig-Standard*, April 4, 1988; Peirol, "1988: A Goodyear for Napanee," *The Whig-Standard*, May 13, 1988; Reid, "Goodyear: A Big Wheel in Business"; *The Toronto Star*, undated; Best, "Hot Goodyear Canada Leaves Shareholders Cold"; and Jeff Outhit, "2,700 Seek 130 Jobs at Goodyear Tire Plant," *The Whig-Standard*, undated, all in AVS, GF. On strike action at Kitchener's Uniroyal-Goodrich plants, see Palmer, *Working-Class Experience*, p.393. The centrality of the new Napanee operation to Goodyear's economic well-being is evident from comments in "Goodyear Canada Slashes Dividend: Tire Maker Reports $13.7m Loss," *The Globe and Mail*, Feb. 23, 1991; "Goodyear Investors Are Licking Their Chops," *The Globe and Mail*, April 20, 1991; "Hot Stocks: Four Picks for the Year Ahead," *Financial Times of Canada*, June 17-23, 1991; "Goodyear To Boost Tire Output: Plans for Napanee Plant May Raise Cost of Acquiring Canadian Unit's Share," *The Globe and Mail*, April 7, 1992; "Costs of Expansion Outweighs Sales Rise," *The Financial Post*, May 20, 1988.

3. See Jack Rafter, "Didn't Drive Plant Away," and Paulette Peirol, "NDSS Students Lament Failure To Lure Industry," *The Whig-Standard*, Dec. 12, 1987; Rafter, "Land Deal to Bring 1,500 Jobs to Napanee Collapses," *The Whig-Standard*, Dec. 10, 1987; Geddes, "Making of the Big Time in a Small Town."

4. Rafter, "Didn't Drive Plant Away"; Peirol, "NDSS Students Lament Failure To

Lure Industry"; Rafter, "Land Deal To Bring 1,500 Jobs to Napanee Collapses." It may well have been known that Goodyear was the company scouting for land, although surprisingly few sources suggest this. A rare exception is the report of a statement by Kingston mayor John Gerretson: "There has been speculation for months that the land was being assembled by Goodyear." See "Goodyear Assembles Land for Plant near Kingston," *The Financial Post*, March 25, 1988.

5. Geddes, "Making of the Big Time in a Small Town"; Paulette Peirol, "Goodyear Announcement Triggers Real-Estate Boom," *The Whig-Standard*, April 23, 1988; Peirol, "Goodyear-Napanee Nuptials Transform Town," *The Whig-Standard*, Dec. 31, 1988; Supplement to *Napanee Beaver*, April 18, 1990.

6. See Paulette Peirol, "Napanee Candidate Hits Paydirt in Land Deal in Neighboring Township," *The Whig-Standard*, Oct. 12, 1988; Peirol, "Nearly $7 Million Offered for Napanee-Area Acreage in One-Company Land Rush," *The Whig-Standard*, Sept. 24, 1988; Jack Rafter, "Toronto Firm Joins Real-Estate Rush, Plans Second Napanee Mall," *The Whig-Standard*, Oct. 11, 1988; James MacArthur, "Goodyear Brings Hope for Future, Planning Problems in Interim," *Napanee Beaver*, Jan. 4, 1989; Jack Rafter, "Banks Requesting Bankruptcy Against Mernick," *The Whig-Standard*, June 20, 1991.

7. Cheryl Boates, "The Region's Newest Plant Confident of Future Growth," *Napanee Beaver*, May 30, 1990; Shelley Aylesworth-Spink to Palmer, Feb. 23, 1993; Jack Rafter, "Kingston Machine Plant Opens Napanee Division," *The Whig-Standard*, May 3, 1990; Ross Lees, "Napanee Development Just Keeps Rolling Along," *Napanee Beaver*, May 30, 1990.

8. Jack Rafter, "Industrial Fever Strikes Napanee, Richmond Area; Negotiations 'Secretive,'" *The Whig-Standard*, May 31, 1989; Chris Malette, "New Business Rumours Circulating," *The Intelligencer* (Belleville), June 22, 1988; Reid, "Goodyear: A Big Wheel in Business"; "Trenton Eyeing Goodyear's Business Spin-offs," *The Intelligencer*, June 22, 1988, in AVS, GF.

9. Shelley Aylesworth-Spink to Palmer, Feb. 23, 1993; Paulette Peirol, "Napanee Land Grab," *The Whig-Standard*, Sept. 24, 1988; Peirol, "Napanee, Neighbors Join Forces to Study Annexation Proposal," *The Whig-Standard*, Sept. 29, 1989; Peirol, "Goodyear-Napanee Nuptials Transform Town"; Peirol, "Residents in Uproar over Subdivision," *The Whig-Standard*, Sept. 22, 1988; James MacArthur, "Goodyear Brings Hope for Future, Planning Problems in Interim," *Napanee Beaver*, Jan. 4, 1989.

10. Paulette Peirol, "Goodyear Neighbors Target Environment," *The Whig-Standard*, April 18, 1988. In the 1970s, Goodyear's Bowmanville plant contracted out the disposal of toxic wastes. The contractor was ill equipped to provide proper disposal, buried 185 forty-five-gallon drums, and was later fined $90,000 and sentenced to jail for thirty days. Goodyear received a verbal reprimand from the judge. See Alan Capon, "Prince Edward County Man Jailed for Burying Toxic Waste Barrels," *The Whig-Standard*, June 23, 1990; Jack Rafter, "Contractor Guilty of Dumping Toxins," *The Whig-Standard*, May 18, 1990. Upon appeal the fine and jail terms were reduced. In May 1994 the convicted contractor, George Crowe, and Goodyear Tire and Rubber Company of

Canada were again in court over the earlier charges of illegal waste disposal. Both Crowe and Goodyear faced common nuisance charges under the Criminal Code following an eighteen-month investigation by the Picton detachment of the Ontario Provincial Police. See Michael Jiggins, "Crowe Dumping Case Enters Second Round," *The Sunday Beaver* (Napanee), May 1, 1994. Goodyear's Owen Sound operation, which makes belts for automobile engines, was closed in the fall of 1990 after tests indicated that potentially carcinogenic polychlorinated biphenyls, or PCBs, had leaked into Lake Huron. The source of the PCBs remained unknown. See "Goodyear Plant Open after PCB Incident," *The Financial Post*, Aug. 31, 1990.

11. Paulette Peirol, "'Pat Answers,' Secrecy Prompts Call for Impact Study," *The Whig-Standard*, June 4, 1988; "Still Negotiating, Goodyear Holds Public Drop-in Sessions," *The Whig-Standard*, April 13, 1988.

12. Harvey Schachter, "The Goodyear Shuffle," *The Whig-Standard*, April 6, 1988; H.W. Webster, letter to the editor, *The Whig-Standard*, April 16, 1988; "We'll Welcome You Here, Goodyear!" *Napanee Beaver*, April 20, 1988; *The Whig-Standard*, July 11, 1988.

13. "Without the Efforts of Certain Persons, Where Would We Be?" *Napanee Beaver*, April 6, 1988; Geddes, "Making of the Big Time in a Small Town." Napanee businessman Bruce McPherson had to reassure Goodyear's U.S. executives that the company truly was wanted. "They had some concerns about the acceptance in the community," he noted. "I think they had misinterpreted what was in the press." See Reid, "Goodyear: A Big Wheel in Business."

5. Enter Education:
Student Power and the Napanee District Secondary School

1. Paulette Peirol, "NDSS Students Lament Failure To Lure Industry," *The Whig-Standard*, Dec. 12, 1987; "Job-starved Napanee Tipped as Goodyear Site," *The Toronto Star*, March 25, 1988; Jack Rafter, "Didn't Drive Plant Away, Hold-out Landowners Say," *The Whig-Standard*, Dec. 12, 1987; Karen Snowdon (Grade 12, NDSS), "Students Use Video To Sell Napanee," *The Whig-Standard*, April 20, 1988; interview with Rod Hughes, Feb. 3, 1989. Hughes told me that the students wanted to protest at the Milligan home, but this was denied by Student Council president Mark Arsenault. Interview with Mark Arsenault, Kingston, March 22, 1993.

2. Peirol, "NDSS Students Lament Failure To Lure Industry"; Napanee District Secondary School, *Student Assembly Video*, NDSS Library, Dec. 11, 1987.

3. Jack Rafter, Paulette Peirol, Bill Hutchison, and Adam Corelli, "Students Sold Us on Napanee" *The Whig-Standard*, March 26, 1988; *Napanee Beaver*, April 6 and June 22, 1988; Shawn Pankow, "Students Played a Key Role!" *Napanee Beaver*, March 30, 1988; Maxine Hagerman, "Napanee Will Never Be the Same: Buzby," and Shawn Pankow, "NDSS Fits Goodyear's Needs 'to a Tee,'" *Napanee Beaver*, May 18, 1988; Geddes, "Making of the Big Time in a Small Town"; Peirol, "1988: A Goodyear for Napanee"; Cathy Hunter, "Goodyear ...," unidentified press clipping (possibly from *The Intelligencer*), in AVS, GF;

interview with Mark Arsenault, Kingston, March 22, 1993; *Student Assembly Video*. On Buzby, see the brief biographical sketch in *Goodyear Canada Inc.: The First 75 Years*, p.124. The April 1993 *Venture* TV program featured O'Connor and his replacement Dick Hopkins, both of whom stressed the tangible value of making NDSS "an industrial training centre."

4. This discussion draws on an interview with Mark Arsenault, Kingston, March 22, 1993; and interview with Terence Murray, Napanee, April 14, 1993. The importance of Guidance Counsellor Murray is almost always ignored. See, however, Snowdon, "Students Use Video to Sell Napanee." Arsenault and Murray confirm each other's accounts, although they differ slightly as to the timing of the Murray-Student Council meeting, Murray placing it at 11:30 A.M. and Arsenault at 2:00-2:30 P.M. They also have different recollections of who actually suggested a student assembly and of when the students saw Hughes and McNamee; neither point, to my mind, is of great importance. NDSS technician Mike Murphy says he videotaped the assembly on his own initiative. He "heard there was to be an assembly" and went home and got his own equipment and was ready the next morning. Telephone conversation with Mike Murphy, April 8, 1993. Most students were undoubtedly quickly swept up in the importance of the NDSS Student Council role in getting Goodyear to come to Napanee; interview with Karen Randall (Grade 9 student in 1987), Newburgh, April 9, 1993.

5. Reid, "Goodyear: A Big Wheel in Business"; *Industrial Data Manual for the Town of Napanee*, VF, NPL.

6. Interview with Rod Hughes, Feb. 3, 1987; phone conversation with Hughes, March 8, 1993. PROJECT THINK files from Hughes and NDSS. It appears that the categories used in creating PROJECT THINK and the Pyramid of Success were borrowed and adapted from Northwest Tech, the school in Lawton, Oklahoma, which provided a detailed "Employability Profile" for students.

7. Peter Hennesy, "What Happens to Individualism When Goodyear Goes to School in Napanee," *The Whig-Standard*, Jan. 21, 1989; Peirol, "'Pat Answers'"; interview with Rod Hughes, Feb. 3, 1989; interview with Karen Randall, April 9, 1993.

8. Interview with Mike Dollack, Principal, NDSS, March 8, 1993.

9. Interview with Rod Hughes, Feb. 3, 1989; interview with Mike Dollack, March 8, 1993; PROJECT FOCUS material provided by Hughes, NDSS. Dollack also stressed NDSS programs that enhanced apprenticeship training possibilities, such as the Secondary School Work Apprenticeship Program, and noted that NDSS is represented on the local Business, Education, and Industry Council, which organizes job fairs and other work-related events. For the business concern with education see Jennifer Lewington, "Business Group Calls for Standard Act," *The Globe and Mail*, March 24, 1993.

10. Interview with Rod Hughes, Feb. 3, 1989; all FIRE documents provided by Hughes, NDSS.

11. Interview with Rod Hughes, Feb. 3, 1989; interview with Mike Dollack, March 8, 1993.

12. Paul Willis, *Learning to Labor: How Working Class Kids Get Working Class Jobs* (New York: Columbia University Press, 1981), p.216. Willis's writing addresses youthful cultures of resistance. In another text he argues perceptively and in ways that seem directly applicable to NDSS: "In so far as education/training becomes ever more subordinated to technical instrumentalism and to the 'needs' of industry, it will be seen as a necessary evil to be tolerated in order to obtain access to the wage in order to obtain access to leisure and consumption and their cultural energies.... Just because the international tide of 'new realism' in education/training correctly perceived and exploited most young people's boredom with and frequent resistance to liberal humanist and traditional approaches is no reason for us to agree that *everything* which is not technical or work oriented should be jettisoned. This is a most alarming jump back through a hundred years of educational reform, a jump which goes in the very *opposite* direction to the movement of common culture, so ensuring, ironically, the further marginalization of even vocational schooling experiences to 'real life', or what most pupils regard as such." Paul Willis, *Common Culture: Symbolic Work at Play in the Everyday Cultures of the Young* (Boulder and San Francisco: Westview Press, 1990), p.147.

13. Interview with Karen Randall, April 9, 1993.

14. Interview with Rod Hughes, Feb. 3, 1989; interview with Mike Dollack, March 8, 1993; Paulette Peirol, "Goodyear to Train Future Workers in Napanee High School," *The Whig-Standard*, July 12, 1988; Jack Rafter and Glen Allen, "Goodyear Name, Colors Dot Hats, Pins, Balloons," *The Whig-Standard*, July 14, 1988; Paulette Peirol, "$130,000 from Skills Quinte Clinches Goodyear Job-Training," *The Whig-Standard*, Sept. 23, 1988; Peirol, "Goodyear-Napanee Nuptials Transform Town"; "Goodyear Hiring Instructors," *Napanee and District Weekly Guide*, Sept. 7, 1988; undated advertisement for two instructors (electrical/electronics), one instructor (hydraulics, pneumatics, mechanics), and two half-time instructors (welding and machine shop) for the "Napanee Goodyear Industrial Maintenance Program," *The Whig-Standard*, in AVS, GF. The training programs fit well with the evolving Conservative Party federal response to economic restructuring and global competition. The Labour Force Development Strategy announced in April 1989, and signalled by the federal government's Supply and Services Canada publications, *Adjusting to Win: Report of the Advisory Council on Adjustment* and *Success in the Works*, shifted federal labour market policy in the training realm away from issues of equity (which had focused, for instance, on women or the disadvantaged) towards efficiency (skills upgrading and skills enhancement). New money, however, was not pumped into this programmatic shift. Rather, an appropriation of $775 million from the Unemployment Insurance program sustained the changing balance of Tory training initiatives. For a fuller discussion, see Rianne Mahon, "Adjusting to Win: The New Tory Training Initiative," in Katherine Graham, ed., *How Ottawa Spends: 1990-1991* (Ottawa: Carleton University Press, 1990), pp.87-113. On student discontent and parking, interview with Karen Randall, April 9, 1993.

15. Paulette Peirol, "Goodyear to Start Accepting Job Applications on November 12," *The Whig-Standard*, "Goodyear Expects 5,000 Applications," *Napanee Beaver*,

and Jeff Outhit, "2,700 Seek 130 Jobs at Goodyear Tire Plant," *The Whig-Standard*, all undated; and M. Patricia Burns, Manager, Employment and Benefits, Goodyear Canada, Inc., to Adrian Van Asseldonk, Manager, Canada Employment Centre, Napanee, May 1, 1992; all in AVS, GF. Paulette Peirol, "Goodyear Attracts 1,000-plus Workers for 60 Job Openings," *The Whig-Standard*, Nov. 14, 1988; Janet Kempenaar, "2,500 Apply for 400 Goodyear Jobs," *Napanee and District Weekly Guide*, April 4, 1989; "Goodyear Plant Announces Hiring of First 60 People," *Napanee Beaver*, Nov. 2, 1988; Derek Baldwin, "2,500 Goodyear Applicants Waiting for a Phone Call," *Napanee Beaver*, April 5, 1989; Ross Lees, "Napanee Plant Breaks Vicious Recession Cycle," *Napanee Beaver*, April 8, 1992; Christina Dona, "1,300 Vie for 400 Tire Plant Jobs," *The Ottawa Citizen*, April 2, 1989; Paulette Peirol, "Doughnuts Outnumber People at Goodyear Job Rush," and "N.D.S.S. Opens for Goodyear Applicants at 5:30 A.M.," *The Whig-Standard*, April 3, 1989; "2700 Line Up for Jobs: Applicants Wait All Night," *The Globe and Mail*, April 27, 1992; "2700 Seek Tire Jobs in Napanee," *Calgary Herald*, April 26, 1992; "Goodyear to Hire," *The Financial Post*, April 7, 1992.

16. Interview with Mike Dollack, March 8, 1993; interview with Terrence Murray, April 14, 1993; "Goodyear of Napanee Receives Highest Award from General Motors Canada," *Napanee and District Weekly Guide*, Oct. 13, 1992. In 1994 Dick Hopkins was acknowledged as being among Canada's best teachers when he became one of the first recipients of the Prime Minister's Awards for Teaching Excellence in Science, Technology and Mathematics. Treated to four days of celebrity status in Ottawa and a cheque for $7,000, Hopkins was feted for his success in conveying to students "what the real world is like." According to reports, his hands-on technical program and its relationship to Goodyear and other corporations were what drew the attention of the state. See *The Whig-Standard*, Feb. 10, 1994.

17. *Tire Tracks*, Feb. 1, 1993 (picture and caption), p.4; "The Real World: Goodyear, Local High School Form Unique Relationship," *Tire Tracks*, June 8, 1992, p.1. Also interview with Mike Dollack, March 8, 1993; telephone conversation with Shelley Aylesworth-Spink, March 1, 1993. *Tire Tracks* is an internal company publication, promoting the Goodyear ideology of familialism, which has apparently been published for a number of years. I was denied complete access to its issues by Aylesworth-Spink, who nevertheless did provide me with copies of material from two issues relating to NDSS.

18. For different approaches to the historically contextualized notion of "the gift," see Gareth Stedman Jones, "The Deformation of the Gift: The Problem of the 1860s," in *Outcast London: A Study in the Relationship Between Classes in Victorian Society* (Harmondsworth, England: Penguin, 1984), pp.241-61; Ian McKay, "'By Wisdom, Wile or War': The Provincial Workmen's Association and the Struggle for Working-Class Independence in Nova Scotia, 1879-1897," *Labour/Le Travail*, 18 (Fall 1986), pp.17-39.

6. Tithing Tire Production:
or, the Goodyear Squeaky Wheel Gets State Oil

1. Shelley Aylesworth-Spink to Palmer, Feb. 23, 1993.

2. These paragraphs draw upon "Major Tire Plant Coming to Area, Minister Says," *The Whig-Standard*, March 24, 1988; "It's (Almost) Definitely Napanee," *The Whig-Standard*, March 25, 1988; Reid, "Goodyear: A Big Wheel in Business"; Paulette Peirol, "County Council Urges Public Support of Goodyear," *The Whig-Standard*, April 15, 1988; Shawn Pankow, "County Eager To Get Wheels Turning," *Napanee Beaver*, April 20, 1988; "Goodyear Seen Waiting for Federal Move on New Tire Plant," *The Globe and Mail*, March 26, 1988; "New Tire Plant Said Up in the Air," *The Globe and Mail*, March 25, 1988. So eager to revitalize the apparently collapsing tire industry was the Ontario government that officials met with corporate leaders outside the province in Europe, Japan, and the United States. See "Goodyear Canada to Build Factory at Napanee," *The Financial Post*, May 13, 1988.

3. Peirol, "MPP: If I Was Napanee I'd Want Some Guarantees"; Peirol, "Goodyear Defends Stepped-up Payments to US," *The Whig-Standard*, May 4, 1988; Clyde Graham, "Federal Remissions to Goodyear Plant 'Unconscionable,' MP Says," *The Whig-Standard*, June 30, 1988; "Etobicoke MP Attacks Ottawa for Aiding Goodyear Despite Layoffs," *The Toronto Star*, June 30, 1988; D.W. Dorken, "Boyer Urges Court Action over Goodyear Perk," *Etobicoke Guardian*, July 6, 1988, in Goodyear Employee Assistance Committee, *Report from the Goodyear Assistance Committee of Goodyear Canada Inc. and Agents of the Salaried Employees and United Rubber Workers of America, Local 232* (Toronto: 1988), in DBF; "Ottawa Offers Enticements for Tire Makers," *The Globe and Mail*, Jan. 8, 1988; Clyde Graham, "Goodyear Getting Break of $38 Million on Duties," *The Whig-Standard*, June 29, 1988; Patricia Lush, "Goodyear To Build Tire Plant in Napanee," *The Globe and Mail*, May 13, 1988; Hagerman, "Could Be a Goodyear for Area!"; "It's Official! Goodyear's Rolling in," *Napanee Beaver*, May 18, 1988; "Goodyear Canada to Build Factory at Napanee." On the stockholder protest over the levy to Akron headquarters, see "Fight over Goodyear Levy," *The Financial Post*, March 17, 1988; "Goodyear Shareholders Trying To Deflate Levy," *The Financial Post*, April 21, 1988; "Goodyear Shareholders Lash 'Levy,'" *The Financial Post*, April 21, 1988; "Goodyear Holder Angry about Proposal to Pay Parent More," *The Globe and Mail*, April 21, 1988; "Levy by Goodyear to Be Investigated," *The Globe and Mail*, April 28, 1988; James Daw, "Goodyear's Shareholders Irked by Plan to Pay Parent," *The Toronto Star*, April 21, 1988.

4. "Goodyear Stays Silent on Levy," *The Financial Post*, May 24, 1988; "Ottawa Unconcerned by Fees to Goodyear," *The Globe and Mail*, May 26, 1988. A year later the stockholder protest had dissipated. See "Goodyear Still Defends Parent's Fee," *The Globe and Mail*, April 20, 1989. See, as well, "Global Competition Overtook New Toronto Capabilities, Hearing Told," *The Wingfoot Clan*, January-February 1987, in DBF; Goodyear Employee Assistance Committee, *Report*, p.18.

5. Peirol, "Honda Town Helps Napanee Plan for Goodyear"; "Financing Set for Goodyear Napanee Plant," *The Globe and Mail*, Jan. 16, 1989; "Duty Extended for Four Tire Makers: Move Will Save Industry $92 Million," *The Globe and Mail*, July 22, 1992; "Tire Makers Get a Break," *The Financial Post*, Sept. 23, 1992. The tire industry appears to do rather well when it comes to government handouts. Michelin, for instance, received $15 million in federal subsidies when it located in Pictou, Nova Scotia, not to mention tax remissions, a provincial loan of $50 million at well below prevailing interest rates, and a $9 million grant. See David Lewis, *Louder Voices: The Corporate Welfare Bums* (Toronto: James Lewis and Samuel, 1972), p.9, a book that gives a general account of the degree and range of state subsidies to multinational corporations.

6. Hagerman, "Napanee Will Never Be the Same"; Hagerman, "Could Be a Goodyear for Area!"; Reid, "Goodyear: A Big Wheel in Business."

7. The Goodyear Family: Union without a UNION

1. For histories of Local 232, see *A Brief History of Local 232, United Rubber, Cork, Linoleum and Plastic Workers of America: 25th Anniversary, 1942-1967* (Toronto, 1967); J. La Force and G. Des Roche, *Local 232, U.R.W.: 40 Years of Progress, Security, Dignity, Equality (June 1 1942—June 1 1982)* (Toronto, 1982).

2. Peirol, "MPP: If I Was Napanee Mayor I'd Want Some Guarantees"; Peter Gorrie, "Goodyear Said Planning Plant to Employ 800 in Eastern Ontario," *The Toronto Star*, undated, in AVS, GF; interview with Vic Cosic and David Birrell, Rubberworkers' Hall, Etobicoke, March 26, 1993; Goodyear Employee Assistance Committee, *Report*. Background on the distinctive industrial, working-class character of Etobicoke is provided in Susan Meurer, "Report on Feasibility Study for Counselling/Advocacy Service in Etobicoke (CASE)," mimeo, May 1990.

3. "Major Tire Plant Coming to Area, Minister Says"; "Still Negotiating, Goodyear Holds Public Drop-in Sessions"; Clyde Graham, "Federal Remissions to Goodyear Plant 'Unconscionable', MP Says," *The Whig-Standard*, June 30, 1988; Peirol, "MPP: If I was Napanee Mayor"; John Deverell, "Plant Closings Set Off Alarm Bells," *The Toronto Star*, March 8, 1987; "Ontario Told To Seek Priority Hiring Pledge," *The Globe and Mail*, March 26, 1988; Goodyear Employee Assistance Committee, *Report*, p.18.

4. This section draws on: interview with Vic Cosic and David Birrell, March 25, 1993; "New Toronto and Goodyear Growing Together: 50 Years of Progress," and "Global Competition Overtook New Toronto Capabilities, Hearing Told," *The Wingfoot Clan*, January-February 1987, in DBF; *Goodyear Canada Inc.: The First 75 Years*; Deverell, "Plant Closings"; and, especially, *The Wingfoot Clan*, May-June 1987, Appendix 15 in Goodyear Employee Assistance Committee, *Report*. On rollerskating: Susan Meurer to Bryan Palmer, Aug. 9, 1993. For brief comment on Goodyear's early paternalism, see James Naylor, *The New Democracy: Challenging the Social Order in Industrial Ontario, 1914-25* (Toronto: University of Toronto Press, 1992), pp.18, 165-66, 170-80.

5. La Force and Des Roche, *Local 232, U.R.W.*; telephone interview with Vic Cosic, March 19, 1993; interview with Cosic and David Birrell, Etobicoke, March 25, 1993; "Goodyear Workers Accept Three-Year Pact," *The Toronto Star*, April 18, 1983. For the 1946 strike, which involved a total of ten thousand Ontario rubberworkers, see Stuart Marshall Jamieson, *Times of Trouble: Labour Unrest and Industrial Conflict in Canada, 1900-66* (Ottawa: Queen's Printer, 1968), p.298.

6. Telephone interview with Vic Cosic, March 19, 1993; interview with Cosic and David Birrell, March 25, 1993; Deverell, "Plant Closings."

7. "Goldsmith Steps Up Activity with Foray on Goodyear Shares," *The Globe and Mail*, Nov. 6, 1986; "The Financier Goodyear Bought Off," *The Globe and Mail*, Nov. 25, 1986. The Goldsmith takeover bid is alluded to in the popularly pitched Harvey H. Segal, *Corporate Makeover: The Reshaping of the American Economy* (New York: Viking, 1989), p.95.

8. Terry Oblander, "Union Locals to Support Lobby Effort: Mercer Says Law Is Faulty on Takeovers," *Akron Beacon Journal*, Nov. 12, 1986; Eric Sandstrom, "Bowlers Take Aim at Goldsmith: Goodyear League Talks Takeover amid the Frames," *Akron Beacon Journal*, Nov. 12, 1986; "The Goodyear Takeover Story: Letters," *Akron Beacon Journal*, Nov. 12, 1986; "Opposite Turn Is Fair Play for Goodyear: Letters," *Akron Beacon Journal*, Nov. 12, 1986, all in DBF; interview with Vic Cosic and David Birrell, March 25, 1993; "Goldsmith Tells Congress Committee Goodyear Needs New Management," *The Globe and Mail*, Nov. 19, 1986; "Goldsmith Gives Up Attempt to Takeover Goodyear," *The Globe and Mail*, Nov. 21, 1986.

9. Oblander, "Union Locals"; "Embattled Goodyear Warns Layoffs Coming," *The Globe and Mail*, Nov. 8, 1986; "Goldsmith Tells Congress Committee Goodyear Needs New Management," *The Globe and Mail*, Nov. 19, 1986; "Goodyear Executive Backs Anti-Takeover Legislation," *The Globe and Mail*, Feb. 20, 1987.

10. "The Financier Goodyear Bought Off," *The Globe and Mail*, Nov. 25, 1986; "Goodyear Revamping Boosts Balance Sheet," *The Globe and Mail*, Jan. 20, 1986; "Warring Sides Claim Credit for Goodyear Rally," *The Globe and Mail*, June 19, 1987; James Buchan, "Goodyear Braces Itself for New Overseas Exports," *The Financial Post*, May 17, 1988; Robert Fernandez, "Dallas Raider Denies Interest in Goodyear," *Akron Beacon Journal*, May 17, 1989 and Gene G. Marcial, "The Big Wheels That May Be after Goodyear," *Inside Wall Street*, June 7, 1989, both in DBF; "The Smoke Clears in Akron: Akron, Ohio Has Lost Its Crown as Tire Capital of the World," *The Globe and Mail*, July 11, 1991; "Goodyear Posts Big Loss: Plans to Lop 3,000 Jobs," *The Globe and Mail*, Oct. 26, 1990; "Goodyear Slashing 1,100 Jobs," *The Globe and Mail*, March 14, 1991; "Goodyear Counting on Profit," *The Globe and Mail*, April 9, 1991; "Goodyear Tire Chairman Resigns: Loss Plagued Company Names Former Rubbermaid Chief as Replacement," *The Globe and Mail*, June 5, 1991; "Banks Give Goodyear Line of Credit," *The Globe and Mail*, Dec. 11, 1986; O'Reilly, *Goodyear Story*, p.149; "Goodyear Sells Its Film Business," *Canadian Packaging*, 45 (May 1992), p.35; "Goodyear Unit Sold," *The Financial Post*, April 9, 1992; "Goodyear Plans Sale [of polyester business] to Shell Canada," *The Globe and Mail*, March

28, 1992; "Goodyear Selling Plant: Huntsman in Line for Toronto Assets," *The Globe and Mail*, April 9, 1992; "Goodyear Cuts Hit Boss's Son," *The Globe and Mail*, April 2, 1992.

11. "To All Employees from R.E. Mercer, Distributed by Akron," Nov. 20, 1986, and "Scott H. Buzby to Dear Employee," Nov. 21, 1986, both in DBF; interview with Vic Cosic and David Birrell, March 25, 1993; "Goodyear Shutdown Wipes out 1557 Jobs," *The Toronto Star*, Nov. 22, 1986.

12. "Goodyear Closing Plant in Toronto," *The Globe and Mail*, Nov. 22, 1986; "Goodyear Will Probably Cut Exports," *The Globe and Mail*, Nov. 25, 1986; "Goodyear Executive Backs Anti-Takeover Legislation," *The Globe and Mail*, Feb. 20, 1987; Deborah Wilson, "Goodyear Workers Face Bleak Future," *The Globe and Mail*, Nov. 24, 1986. Union officials confirmed that there was, by the mid-to-late 1980s, "no real head office Canada control, except over the retail outlets. Akron has centralized everything." Interview with Vic Cosic and David Birrell, March 25, 1993.

13. For the stock wars of this period, see "Goodyear Canada Trades below Book," *Investors Digest*, 18 (Sept. 9, 1986), p.269; "Goodyear Studying Share Offering in Canada," *The Globe and Mail*, April 9, 1987; "A Hot Time's Expected at Goodyear Meeting," *The Financial Post*, April 20, 1988; "Goodyear Draws Ire of Minority Investors," *The Financial Post*, March 23, 1988; "Goodyear Minority Puts Gloves On," *The Financial Post*, April 14, 1988; Edward Clifford, "Goodyear Investors Are Licking Their Chops," *The Globe and Mail*, April 20, 1991; "Goodyear Canada Stocks Soars: Investors Like Buyout Offer," *The Financial Post*, Feb. 22-24, 1992; "Goodyear Tire to Buy Up Canadian Division's Shares," *The Globe and Mail*, Feb. 21, 1992; "Goodyear Battle Looming: Buyout Offer Boosts Stock," *The Globe and Mail*, Feb. 26, 1992; "Shareholders Feel Shortchanged: Goodyear Canada's Tax Loss Credits Total $106.7 M," *The Globe and Mail*, May 22, 1992; "Goodyear to Boost Tire Output: Plans for Napanee Plant May Raise Cost of Acquiring Canadian Unit's Shares," *The Globe and Mail*, April 7, 1992; Best, "Hot Goodyear Canada Leaves Shareholders Cold"; "Goodyear Canada Inc Board Approves Goodyear Tire & Rubber Co Buyout," *The Globe and Mail*, May 14, 1992; "Goodyear Deal," *The Financial Post*, May 14, 1992; "Goodyear Shareholders Reject Offer," *The Financial Post*, June 24, 1992; "Proxy Fight Nears Climax: Bone of Contention Is What Goodyear Wants to Pay," *The Financial Post*, June 20-22, 1992; "Goodyear Buyout Bid Faces Rejection: Shareholders Poke Holes in $48 Offer," *The Globe and Mail*, June 23, 1992; "Goodyear Buyout Offers Rejected: Shareholders Want More than $48, but Company Says Bid Won't Be Bumped Up," *The Globe and Mail*, June 24, 1992; "Why Davids Confounded a Goliath," *The Financial Post*, June 26, 1992; "Davids Can Deliver the Goods," *The Financial Post*, April 12, 1991; Edward Clifford, "A Way to Sweeten Goodyear Offer," *The Globe and Mail*, July 15, 1992; "Minority Interests Flex Their Muscles," *The Financial Post*, Aug. 29-31, 1992. Goodyear Canada's March 1993 stock quote from *The Globe and Mail*, March 23, 1993.

14. John Deverell, "Plant Closings."

15. Deborah Wilson, "Goodyear Workers Face Bleak Future"; interview with Vic

Cosic and David Birrell, March 25, 1993; Christie Blatchford, "They Lost More Than Their Jobs," *The Toronto Star,* undated, and "Buzby to Dear Employee," Nov. 21, 1986, both in DBF; Carol Matlack, "Forewarning: Canada's Experience with Mandatory Plant-Closing Notice Has Not Been the Debacle Opponents Once Warned Of," *National Journal,* June 11, 1988, p.1537, in Appendix 14, "Newspaper Clippings," Goodyear Employee Assistance Committee, *Report.* On the matter of outgoing machinery, graffiti, and worker anger I rely on Susan Meurer to Bryan Palmer, Aug. 9, 1993. As a counsellor to the laid-off Goodyear employees, Meurer was given a tour of the plant during its last days.

16. Duncan McMonagle, "NDP to Press for Review of Decision to Close Plant," *The Globe and Mail,* Nov. 24, 1986; "Not Optimistic Goodyear Jobs Can Be Saved," *The Toronto Star,* Nov. 25, 1986; "Goodyear Again Refuses Offer to Help to Build New Tire Plant," *The Toronto Star,* Nov. 26, 1986; "Aid Offers Will Not Change Decision," *The Globe and Mail,* Nov. 25, 1986; "Ontario Willing to Save Jobs at Goodyear, O'Neil Insists," *The Toronto Star,* Nov. 28, 1986; "Province, Employees Might Buy the Plant," *The Toronto Star,* Nov. 27, 1986; Wilson, "Goodyear Workers Face Bleak Future"; "Global Competition Overtook New Toronto Capabilities, Hearing Told"; "Goodyear Plans 1,000-Job Plant," *The Toronto Star,* Feb. 20, 1987; Deverell, "Plant Closings"; "Goodyear Studying Share Offering in Canada." It is tempting to see Goodyear's 1986-87 statements on the banks and Goldsmith as a subdued, late-twentieth century variant of the rhetorical populist/patrician anti-semitism of earlier periods in U.S. history. If this is indeed the case, and it may well be, Goodyear officials avoid direct anti-semitic statements. See Richard Hofstadter, *The Paranoid Style in American Politics and Other Essays* (New York: Vintage, 1967); and Richard Hofstadter, *The Age of Reform: From Bryan to F.D.R.* (New York: Vintage, 1955).

17. Blatchford, "They Lost More Than Their Jobs"; Gigi Suhanic, "Goodyear's Getaway," *Now,* Nov. 19-25, 1987; Wilson, "Goodyear Workers Face Bleak Future"; Deverell, "Plant Closings"; "500 Goodyear Staff Finish Last Shift: Many Fear No Jobs for Unemployed Tire Workers," *The Toronto Star,* May 2, 1987.

18. Blatchford, "They Lost More Than Their Jobs" and "United Rubber, Cork, Linoleum and Plastic Workers to Dear Member," April 1, 1987, in DBF; "Laid-off Tire Workers Find Job Hunt Leads Mostly to Dead Ends," *The Globe and Mail,* undated, and Carol Matlack, "Forewarning," *National Journal,* June 11, 1988, pp.1534-1537, both in Appendix 14, "Newspaper Clippings," Goodyear Employee Assistance Committee, *Report*; Deverell, "Plant Closings." The heavily funded state-orchestrated assistance committee sponsored a counselling program, run out of Humber College, that addressed the job training and language needs of the laid-off Goodyear workers, seventy-eight of whom participated in the program. See Susan Meurer (co-ordinator), "Goodyear Transition Project—Final Report Prepared for the Employee Adjustment Branch of the Ontario Ministry of Labour," mimeo, for Craig Barrett, Humber College, Toronto. Meurer and others—including unionist David Birrell and NDP member Ruth Grier—then tried to extend the success of the Goodyear employee assistance program (out of which came models of job-search techniques and

English-as-a-second-language training used across Canada) into a generalized, permanent service for older, displaced workers in the Etobicoke-Lakeshore areas. After securing funding for a feasibility study, completion of Meurer's initial report, establishment of a participatory advisory committee, and a beginning service, run out of the URW hall, the program got derailed, the original committee was dismantled, counsellors were judged unqualified, and the union hall was abandoned as the site of assistance. What remained was appropriated and bureaucratized by the state-run Canada Employment Centre machinery. See Meurer, "Report on Feasibility Study," and Meurer to Palmer, Aug. 9, 1993.

19. This section draws upon sources provided to me by Susan Meurer, whom I met, interestingly, in the Sudbury hall of the Mine, Mill, and Smelter Workers Union, where we were both attending a centenary celebration of one of Canada's more radical labour organizations. I knew of her work with David Sobel: an attempt to preserve the historical record of the John Inglis factory in Toronto, which closed in November 1989. But in the context of living working-class traditions I discovered that Meurer had been one of the counsellors I was reading about in my research on the Goodyear Etobicoke closure and, furthermore, that she had been involved in cultural efforts to translate the meaning of the plant shutdown to workers and wider audiences. "Closure" appeared in the "Connections" section of *Canadian Dimension*, March/April 1988, p.23. *The Shadowboxers*, presented in five episodes on CBC-Radio's *Morningside*, was written by Meurer, with music and lyrics by Allen Booth, produced by Greg Sinclair, and is available on cassette. On the play see also, Mark Curtis, "Play Examines 'Black Cloud' of Plant Closures," *Etobicoke Life*, March 8, 1989. I also draw on two letters from Susan Meurer to myself, undated (May 1993) and May 26, 1993. On the Sobel-Meurer Inglis project, see John Bentley Mays, "Lives on the Line," *The Globe and Mail*, Oct. 7, 1992; and a promotional four-page blurb, "Working at Inglis: 100 Years in a Toronto Factory," courtesy of Susan Meurer. Sobel has also worked on a photographic history of the General Motors van plant in Scarborough, home of Canadian Automobile Workers (CAW) Local 303. See Gayle Hurmuses, "Jobs on the Line: The Last Days of Local 303," *The Globe and Mail*, May 1, 1993; CAW Local 303 Heritage Committee, *You Can't Bring Back Yesterday: A History of CAW Local 303* (Willowdale, 1993).

20. "Goodyear Plan for [Ontario] Plant Upsets Former [Etobicoke] Workers," *The Toronto Star*, March 28, 1988; Blatchford, "They Lost More Than Their Jobs."

21. Deverell, "Plant Closings"; "Former Goodyear Workers Demand New Severance Deal," *The Toronto Star*, March 21, 1987; "500 Goodyear Staff Finish Last Shift"; "Pension Boost Worth 'Millions' Set for Workers at Goodyear," *The Toronto Star*, May 12, 1987; "Ontario Pension Bill Changed to Benefit Goodyear Workers," *Benefits Canada*, 11 (June 1987), pp.5,7; "Workers Mourn at Goodyear's Last Shift," *The Toronto Star*, May 30, 1987; "Notice Local 232 U.R.W.," flyer, Feb. 6, 1987, "Pension Benefits: Mrs. Grier and the Honourable Mr. Kwinter Discussion Re Bill 170," unattributed account of Ontario Legislature session, April 29, 1987, "Submission of Local 232, U.R.C.L. & P.W.U. to the Standing Committee on General Government, Bill 170 to Revise

the Pension Benefits Act," undated, United Rubber, Cork, Linoleum & Plastic Workers, "Goodyear Plant Closure," May 1, 1987 and May 29, 1987, *New Advocate*, Feb. 23, 1987, David Birrell "Address to Brothers and Sisters at 11 May 1987 Demonstration," all in DBF. Harvey Schachter, "The Goodyear Shuffle," *The Whig-Standard*, April 6, 1988; H.W. Webster, "Goodyear Has Been a Good Corporate Citizen," *The Whig-Standard*, April 16, 1988; Cathy Hunter, "Goodyear ...," unidentified clipping (*The Intelligencer* [Belleville]) in AVS, GF. On the Ontario government's legislation, see "Statement in the Legislature by the Honourable Monte Kwinter, Minister of Financial Institutions, Re: An Act to Amend the Pensions Benefits Act, Motions Moved in Committee, May 11, 1987," Toronto. For the arbitration decisions, see "Decision, Kenneth P. Swan Arbitration Limited, Re: The Employment Standards Act Section 51 Hearing, Goodyear Canada Incorporated," Dec. 2, 1988, and "Decision, Kenneth P. Swan, in the Matter of the Employment Standards Act and Goodyear Canada Incorporated dated 26 June 1987," Jan. 16, 1991. The last three unpublished documents are in DBF. Certainly union officials have a sense that everything Goodyear gave on pensions and severance it was forced to give: telephone interview with Vic Cosic, March 19, 1993; interview with Cosic and David Birrell, March 25, 1993.

22. "Plans a $6.1 Million Expansion of Its Plastic Firms Manufacturing Plant," *The Globe and Mail*, Feb. 13, 1987; "Goodyear Plans for Plant Expansion Will Aid Etobicoke," *The Toronto Star*, Feb. 14, 1987; "Goodyear Tire, Developer Reach Sale Agreement on Plant Site," *The Toronto Star*, Sept. 3, 1987; "Goodyear Slashes Price of Property in Etobicoke," *The Toronto Star*, May 3, 1988; "Houses Proposed for Goodyear Site: Developer Hopes for Rezoning," *The Globe and Mail*, Dec. 20, 1988. By 1993 the former Goodyear site was being transformed into an intensively focused community "development" dubbed Lakeshore Village. See Adele Freedman, "A New Community Shaping Up in Etobicoke," *The Globe and Mail*, Oct. 2, 1993.

23. Peirol, "MPP: If I Was Napanee Mayor"; Peirol, "1988: A Goodyear for Napanee"; telephone interview with Vic Cosic, March 19, 1993. Within the Napanee region it was well known that Goodyear intended to keep the plant non-union. Interview with Terence Murray, Napanee, April 14, 1993.

24. Among the many useful statements on the decline of trade unionism, see Michael Goldfield, *The Decline of Organized Labor in the United States* (Chicago: University of Chicago Press, 1987); Kim Moody, *An Injury to All: The Decline of American Unionism* (London: Verso, 1988); Leo Panitch and Donald Swartz, *The Assault on Trade Union Freedoms* (Toronto: Garamond Press, 1988); Jane Jenson and Rianne Mahon, eds., *The Challenge of Restructuring: North American Labor Movements Respond* (Philadelphia: Temple University Press, 1993). For specific comment on deindustrialization and union decline in the Akron-based tire plants, see "Smoke Clears in Akron"; Charles Jeszeck, "Decline of Tire Manufacturing in Akron," in Charles Craypo and Bruce Nissen, eds., *Grand Designs: The Impact of Corporate Strategies on Workers, Unions, and Communities* (Ithaca, N.Y.: Cornell University Press, 1993), pp.18-42. On the URW, see Ken Clare, "Michelin—The Fortress That Didn't Fall," *New Maritimes*, 4 (July-August 1986), pp.4-9. I also draw my assessment of the URW

from telephone interview with Vic Cosic, March 19, 1993; and interview with Cosic and David Birrell, March 25, 1993.

25. O'Reilly, *Goodyear Story*, pp.193-194; "Productivity Gains Not Reflected in Workers' Pay," *The Globe and Mail*, June 19, 1987.

26. O'Reilly, *Goodyear Story*, p.194; Peirol, "1988: A Goodyear for Napanee"; Paulette Peirol, "Illinois 'Farm Boy' Will Be First Goodyear Manager," *The Whig-Standard*, undated, in AVS, GF; "New Manager Named for Goodyear Plant," *Napanee Beaver*, Nov. 2, 1988; Jack Rafter, "Goodyear Names No. 2 Man at Plant," *The Whig-Standard*, Oct. 20, 1988. On Hogeboom, see *The Whig-Standard*, Nov. 28, 1988.

27. On Valleyfield, see "Quebec Workers Strike at Goodyear Tire Plant," *The Globe and Mail*, Jan. 16, 1985; "Goodyear Production Shift [from Valleyfield] Would Cost 300 Jobs," *The Gazette* (Montreal), Feb. 28, 1985; "New Pact May Create 200 Jobs," *The Gazette*, March 1, 1985; "Goodyear Strike Approaches Critical Stage as Talks Resume," *The Globe and Mail*, March 2, 1985; "Labor Woe at Tire Plant Is Continuing," *The Globe and Mail*, March 7, 1985; "Union Hopeful at Goodyear," *The Globe and Mail*, March 15, 1985; "Goodyear Carries Out Threat: Strike-bound Canadian Plant Moved to US," *The Chronicle Herald* (Halifax), March 15, 1985; "Goodyear Shuts Its Strike-Hit Plant," *The Gazette*, March 15, 1985; "Goodyear Threatens to Close Strike-bound Plant," *Winnipeg Free Press*, March 16, 1985; "Vote Ends Goodyear Strike," *The Gazette*, March 25, 1985; "62% Vote Ends Strike at Goodyear," *The Globe and Mail*, March 26, 1985; "Goodyear Cites Strike for Deep Cut in Profit," *The Globe and Mail*, Feb. 13, 1986; "Goodyear Plans to Lay Off 360 from Montreal Plant," *The Whig-Standard*, Aug. 1, 1990; "Goodyear Laying Off 360 Workers at Valleyfield," *The Gazette*, Aug. 1, 1990; "Goodyear Canada Inc Will Lay Off 360 Employees at its Manufacturing Plant West of Montreal," *The Globe and Mail*, Aug. 3, 1990; "Goodyear Canada Inc Workers Get Reprieve from Layoff," *The Globe and Mail*, Sept. 28, 1990; "Goodyear Cuts 100 Jobs in Ontario," *The Globe and Mail*, Sept. 13, 1990; "Goodyear Cutting Production and Staff," *The Globe and Mail*, Sept. 1, 1990; "530 Laid Off at Goodyear: Gulf Crisis, Car Slump Cited," *The Gazette*, Aug. 31, 1990; "Goodyear Lays Off up to 600 Workers: About 30 Affected in Valleyfield," *The Globe and Mail*, June 12, 1991; "Goodyear to Close Quebec Plant, Lay Off 144," *The Globe and Mail*, June 27, 1991; "Goodyear to Shut St. Hyacinthe Plant, 144 to Lose Jobs," *The Gazette*, June 27, 1991; "Goodyear to Cut Jobs," *The Gazette*, April 5, 1991; "Goodyear Recalling 27 Workers," *The Globe and Mail*, Nov. 12, 1991; "Goodyear Recalls 100 Workers," *The Gazette*, Nov. 12, 1991; "Goodyear Starts to Recall 100 Laid Off Workers," *The Toronto Star*, Nov. 12, 1991; "Goodyear Tire and Rubber Co Recalls 300 Workers," *The Globe and Mail*, Feb. 3, 1992; "Goodyear Canada Inc Recalls Valleyfield Workers," *The Globe and Mail*, March 21, 1992. For a study of the Energy and Chemical Workers Union, see Wayne Roberts, *Cracking the Canadian Formula: The Making of the Energy and Chemical Workers Union* (Toronto: Between the Lines, 1990). It is clear from the financial reporting that the Napanee plant was conceived by the early 1990s as a pacesetting operation, shoring up the value of Goodyear. See the stock market commentary on Goodyear in "Hot Stocks: Four Picks of the Year Ahead," *Financial Times of Canada*, June 17-23,

1991; "Goodyear to Boost Tire Output: Plans for Napanee Plant May Raise Cost of Acquiring Canadian Unit's Shares," *The Globe and Mail,* April 7, 1992.

28. For the sorry URW record in Nova Scotia in the 1970s, which involved Vic Cosic, see Ken Clare, "Michelin—The Fortress That Didn't Fall," *New Maritimes,* 4 (July-August 1986), pp.4-8. Telephone interview with Cosic, March 19, 1993; interview with Cosic and David Birrell, March 25, 1993. Gibara is quoted in "Goodyear Expecting to Rebound after Skid," *The Globe and Mail,* April 19, 1990, while Buzby is quoted in Peirol, "1988: A Goodyear for Napanee."

8. Bread, Circuses, and the Blimp

1. *The Whig-Standard,* March 26, 1988, May 13, 1988; "Eastern Ontario in Running for Super Tire Plant," *The Financial Post,* March 24, 1988; "Goodyear to Build Tire Plant in Napanee," *The Globe and Mail,* May 13, 1988; "Napanee to Get $300 M. Tire Plant," *Heavy Construction News,* April 1988; "Tire Plant Reported to Be Built in Ontario," *The Gazette,* March 24, 1988.

2. "Blimp Is on Its Way," *Napanee Beaver,* June 22, 1988.

3. Paulette Peirol, "Goodyear Blimp Is 'Largest Corporate Symbol in the World,'" *The Whig-Standard,* July 6, 1988; Shawn Pankow, "America the Beautiful: Goodwill Ambassador Lifted a Select Few to New Heights," *Napanee Beaver,* July 20, 1988. For more on the Goodyear blimps, see "New Goodyear Blimp Has Bigger Waistline," *Canadian Aviation,* 60 (September 1987), pp.14-15; "Debt Heavy Goodyear Could Ground Blimps," *The Globe and Mail,* July 22, 1991; "Goodyear Blimp Boosts Tire Promo," *Strategy,* 3 (July 27, 1992), p.12.

4. Paulette Peirol, "Goodyear Mandate: Organize a Party for 10,000," *The Whig-Standard,* July 7, 1988; "Blimp Is on Its Way," *Napanee Beaver,* June 22, 1988.

5. Paulette Peirol, "Goodyear Asks 350 VIPS to Sod-Turning Ceremony," *The Whig-Standard,* July 8, 1988; Peirol, "Goodyear Mandate," *The Whig-Standard,* July 7, 1988; *The Whig-Standard,* July 14, 1988.

6. Paulette Peirol, "Mall Merchants Kick in $2,000 for Goodyear Photo Display," *The Whig-Standard,* July 9, 1988; Peirol, "OPP Advise Locals to Leave Car at Home and Walk to Goodyear Friendship Fest," *The Whig-Standard,* July 11, 1988; Jack Rafter and Glen Allen, "Goodyear Name, Colors Dot Hats, Pins, Balloons," *The Whig-Standard,* July 14, 1988; *Napanee Beaver,* July 6, 1988.

7. Paulette Peirol, "Friendship Festival: Goodyear Chooses Children for Sod-Turning Ceremonies," July 4, 1988; Shawn Pankow, "Wheels Turning for July 13 Extravaganza!" *Napanee Beaver,* July 6, 1988; Allyson Latta, "Symbolic Sod-Turning Takes Place in Cloud of Dust as 200 Youngsters Root for Prizes in Huge Sandbox," *The Whig-Standard,* July 14, 1988.

8. Paulette Peirol, "Bash Well Worth $100,000, Company Officials Say," *The Whig-Standard,* July 14, 1988; Pankow, "Wheels Turning for July 13 Extravaganza!"; Maxine Hagerman, "Goodyear's True Colors Shine Through!" and "The Ground's Been Broken ... Let the Work Begin," *Napanee Beaver* (special

edition), July 16, 1988.

9. Peirol, "Bash well worth $100,000"; and Rafter and Allen, "Goodyear name, Colors Dot Hats, Pins, Balloons."

10. Latta, "Symbolic sod-turning"; Peirol, "Bash Well Worth $100,000"; Friendship Festival videotape, July 13, 1988, NDSS Library.

11. Rafter and Allen, "Goodyear Name, Colors Dot Hats, Pins, Balloons"; Allyson Latta and Scott Anderson, "Most Party-Goers Welcome Goodyear with Open Arms," and Scott Anderson, "Napanee's Quiet Pace, Simplicity Win Raves from Head Office Visitors," *The Whig-Standard*, July 14, 1988; Harvey Schachter, "Goodyear's Party," *The Whig-Standard* (editorial) undated, in AVS, GF. David Birrell is quoted in Peirol, "Friendship Festival," while Vic Cosic's presence was acknowledged in telephone interview with Cosic, March 19, 1993; interview with Cosic and David Birrell, Etobicoke, March 25, 1993. Cosic felt the URW had no place in leafleting the ground-breaking ceremony, informing the participants of the plight of Goodyear's Etobicoke workers. "Not a day to leaflet yet, no plant, no building yet," he replied mechanically and unimaginatively.

12. Peirol, "Bash Well Worth $100,000."

13. Paulette Peirol, "Goodyear Says 'Thanks' to Volunteers," *The Whig-Standard*, July 15, 1988; Bill Hodgins, "The Party after the Party," *Napanee Beaver*, July 20, 1988; Rafter and Allen, "Goodyear Name, Colors Dot Hats, Pins, Balloons," *The Whig-Standard*, July 14, 1988; Latta and Anderson, "Most Party-Goers Welcome Goodyear."

14. Maxine Hagerman, "And Wasn't That a Breathtaking Party!" *Napanee Beaver*, July 16, 1988.

15. Hagerman, "Goodyear's True Colors Shine Through!"; "Getting into Gear with Goodyear," *Napanee Beaver* (editorial), July 20, 1988. For a visual account of the July 13, 1988, Friendship Festival, see the videotape made by Mike Murphy, available on the same tape as the student assembly video, Dec. 11, 1987, NDSS Library.

9. The Costs of Construction: Building the World's Most Modern Tire Plant

1. This is perhaps a highly problematic and certainly unorthodox deployment of traditional Marxist categories. It nevertheless seems to have some purchase on the experience of capital and class in Napanee in the late twentieth century. On primitive accumulation, see Karl Marx, *Capital: A Critical Analysis of Capitalist Production*, Vol.1 (New York: International, 1967), pp.713-74. V.I. Lenin's *Imperialism, the Highest Stage of Capitalism* (Peking: Foreign Languages Press, 1965 [1917]), can be read as differentiating colonialism and imperialism, stressing that imperialism is a process of capital export associated with the monopolistic stage of capitalist development. Note, as well, the contentious but important arguments of Bill Warren, *Imperialism: Pioneer of Capitalism* (London: Verso, 1980). Marxist attempts to deal with the cultural, logical, and spatial configuration of late capitalism include Fredric Jameson,

Postmodernism; Or, the Cultural Logic of Late Capitalism (Durham, N.C.: Duke University Press, 1991) and Harvey, *Condition of Postmodernity*.

2. I would like to thank my friend Nick Rogers who, during one of our Thursday night sessions, prodded me to be product-specific with respect to this argument. The line of poetry comes from Ernesto Cardenal, "Oracle over Managua," quoted in Himani Bannerji, "Nostalgia for the Future: The Poetry of Ernesto Cardenal," *The Writing on the Wall: Essays on Culture and Politics* (Toronto: TSAR, 1993), p.5.

3. This represents an entire chapter in recent business history. See, for an introduction, "Goodyear's Strategy," *The Financial Post*, March 15, 1986; "Ads in the Fast Lane," *Marketing*, July 28, 1986; Colin Leduc, "Goodyear Steers in New Directions," *The Financial Post*, Oct. 12, 1987; "Distributor Bought," *The Financial Post*, June 3, 1988; "Goodyear Buys York Tire in 'Friendly' Takeover," *Winnipeg Free Press*, June 2, 1988; "Foster Gets Goodyear," *The Financial Post*, June 14, 1988; "Goodyear Touts Its Tune-ups: Campaign Emphasizes 'We Market More than Tires,'" *Marketing*, April 1, 1991; "Goodyear's One-Stop Service Approach Starting to Catch On," *Motor Truck*, July 1992; "The Chase Is On for Auto Servicing Market," *The Globe and Mail*, Feb. 4, 1992; "Auto Service Newest Development: Goodyear Canada's Strategy for Growth Builds on Tires' Good Name," *Trade and Commerce*, 87 (Spring 1992), pp.P2,10; "Sears to Sell Goodyear," *The Globe and Mail*, March 9, 1992; "Goodyear to Take Quantum Leap [in tire technology]," *The Chronicle Herald*, Sept. 5, 1991; "Goodyear Tirelessly Tuning Up Its Image," *The Globe and Mail*, Jan. 2, 1992; "Flat Run Tires," *The Globe and Mail*, Sept. 8, 1992; "How to Win the Rubber Match," *The Globe and Mail*, Nov. 3, 1992; "Goodyear Foresees Good Profit," *The Globe and Mail*, April 14, 1992.

4. These partial figures, which understate the dimensions of plant closures and job losses, were calculated from two typescripts, "Tire Plant Closings 1973 to Present (United States)," and "Tire Plants in Canada—September 1982-July 1987," both in DBF. For general statements on the tire industry and restructuring, see "Smoke Clears in Akron"; "Foreign Pressures Tighten Pinch on Canada's 'Marginal' Tire Plants," *The Financial Post*, Jan. 25, 1988. On Goodyear's proposed South Korean plant, see "Goodyear in Canada," *Akron Beacon Journal*, April 13, 1988 and "Tire Firms Invest $4 Billion for Expansions," *Rubber and Plastic News*, Oct. 17, 1988, both in DBF.

5. See "Goodyear Sells Zaire Tire Unit," *The Globe and Mail*, May 27, 1987; "Goodyear Pulling Out of South Africa after 42 Years," *The Gazette*, June 8, 1989; "Goodyear Tire Selling South African Operation," *The Globe and Mail*, June 8, 1989; "Goodyear Selling off South African Unit," *The Financial Post*, June 8, 1989; "Goodyear May Fire South African Workers," *The Financial Post*, Aug. 9, 1989; "Goodyear Selling Off Its Operations in South Africa as It Quits Country," *The Toronto Star*, June 8, 1989.

6. This terminology is used quite readily in casual conversations. Rod Hughes alluded to "Japanese management" in 1989, but deflected the negative connotations of the term by suggesting that Goodyear-style management was primarily an attempt to "empower people." Hughes also "Americanized" and legit-

imized such an approach, and its application to education, by locating its origins in Harvard studies. Interview with Rod Hughes, Feb. 3, 1989. In general see Jonathan Morris, "A Japanization of Canadian Industry?" in Drache and Gertler, *New Era of Global Competition*, pp.206-28; Stephen Wood, "Japanization and/or Toyotaism?" *Work, Employment and Society*, 5, 4 (December 1991), pp.567-600; D. Robertson, J. Rinehart, C. Huxley and the CAW Research Group on CAMI, "Team Concept and 'Kaizen': Japanese Production Management in a Unionized Canadian Auto Plant," *Studies in Political Economy*, 39 (Autumn 1992), pp.77-108.

7. Jack Rafter, "Goodyear's A-Rollin'," *The Whig-Standard*, Oct. 19, 1990; Heather Gilchrist, "Flags Fly at Goodyear for Opening," *Napanee Beaver*, Oct. 3, 1990; "Goodyear Expecting to Rebound after Skid," *The Globe and Mail*, April 19, 1990.

8. Rafter, "Goodyear's A-Rollin'."

9. Maxine Hagerman, "Goodyear Unveils Initial Plans for Plant," *Napanee Beaver*, April 20, 1988; "Goodyear Plant on Schedule for 1990 Start-Up," *Loyalist Country Living*, February 1989; James MacArthur, "Goodyear Construction on Schedule," *Napanee Beaver*, Jan. 18, 1989; Gordon Pitts, "A Tale of Two Ontario Companies," *The Financial Post*, July 16, 1990; telephone interview with Vic Cosic, March 19, 1993; interview with Cosic and Dave Birrell, March 25, 1993. Shelley Aylesworth-Spink quoted in "2700 Line Up for Jobs: Eager Applicants Wait All Night," *The Globe and Mail*, April 27, 1992.

10. *Tire Tracks*, June 8, 1992; sticker reading "Goodyear Napanee: 'We Drive For Quality,'" and blue seminar notebook entitled "Tri-balance." Goodyear would not grant me permission to reproduce the imagery in these items.

11. Goodyear Canada Communique, undated, relating to construction as of Jan. 17, 1989, in AVS, GF; MacArthur, "Goodyear Construction on Schedule."

12. Jack Rafter, "Unions Picket Goodyear Site," *The Whig-Standard*, Sept. 23, 1988; Paulette Peirol, "Goodyear Hiring Protest Blamed on Union Dispute," *The Whig-Standard*, Sept. 27, 1988; Peirol, "Unions Attempt to Resolve Goodyear Dispute," *The Whig-Standard*, Sept. 28, 1988; Maxine Hagerman, "Goodyear Site Picketed," *Napanee Beaver*, Sept. 28, 1988.

13. This section draws upon "Construction Accident," *Napanee and District Weekly Guide*, Feb. 7, 1989; Paulette Peirol, "Steelworker Plunges from Goodyear Roof," *The Whig-Standard*, Feb. 6, 1989; Derek Baldwin, "Fall Hurts Worker at Goodyear Site," *Napanee Beaver*, Feb. 8, 1989; James MacArthur, "Coroner's Jury Decides Safety Should Improve," *Napanee Beaver*, May 17, 1989; Paulette Peirol, "Most Construction Deaths Due to Falls, Ministry Says," *The Whig-Standard*, May 11, 1989.

14. Peirol, "Goodyear Attracts 1,000-plus Workers for 60 Job Openings"; Peirol, "Doughnuts Outnumber People"; Derek Baldwin, "2,500 Goodyear Applicants Waiting for a Phone Call," *Napanee Beaver*, April 5, 1989; Latta and Anderson, "Most Party-Goers Welcome Goodyear with Open Arms."

15. O'Reilly, *Goodyear Story*, p.194; Rafter, "Goodyear's A-Rollin'"; Peirol, "Doughnuts Outnumber People"; MacArthur, "Goodyear Construction on Schedule"; interview with Karen Randall, April 9, 1993.

16. Shelley Aylesworth-Spink to Palmer, Feb. 23, 1993; Gordon Pitts, "A Tale of Two Ontario Companies"; Communique Goodyear Canada Inc., undated, but detailing construction stage as of Jan. 17, 1989; interview with Vic Cosic and David Birrell, March 25, 1993. On awards see, "Goodyear of Napanee Receives Highest Award from General Motors Canada," *The Weekly Guide*, Oct. 13, 1992; "About Our Business," *Tire Tracks*, June 8, 1992.

17. K.B. Kleckner, "Around the Plant—Team Appreciation Day: Special People, Special Place," and "Local Notes: Team Appreciation Day Update," in *Tire Tracks*, June 8, 1992. Note that the stress on family and job security has long been central at the Goodyear Lawton plant. In 1989 a worker there stated, "It is more important than wage increases. I am convinced that if the tire market collapses, Lawton will be the last plant to shut down. That is what keeps me going. The big increases will come someday." See "Productivity Gains Not Reflected in Workers' Pay," *The Globe and Mail*, June 19, 1987.

18. O'Reilly, *Goodyear Story*, p.195.

19. Karen Snowdon, "Students Use Video to Sell Napanee," *The Whig-Standard*, April 20, 1988.

10. The Contested Meanings of History

1. *Goodyear Canada Inc.: The First 75 Years*, p.13.

2. Rafter, Peirol, Hutchison, and Corelli, "Students Sold Us on Napanee."

3. Both quotes from Elizabeth Fox-Genovese and Eugene D. Genovese, "The Political Crisis of Social History: Class Struggle as Subject and Object," in *Fruits of Merchant Capital: Slavery and Bourgeois Property in the Rise and Expansion of Capitalism* (Oxford: Oxford University Press, 1983), pp.211-12.

4. Pauline Marie Rosenau, *Post-Modernism and the Social Sciences: Insights, Inroads, and Intrusions* (Princeton, N.J.: Princeton University Press, 1992), p.64; Fredric Jameson, "Postmodernism and Consumer Society," in *The Anti-Aesthetic: Essays on Postmodern Culture*, ed. Hal Foster (Port Townsend, Wash.: Bay Press, 1983), p.125; Jameson, *Postmodernism: Or, the Cultural Logic of Late Capitalism* (Durham, N.C.: Duke University Press, 1991), p.217. For my own views on postmodernism, see Bryan D. Palmer, "The Poverty of Theory Revisited: Or, Critical Theory, Historical Materialism, and the Ostensible End of Marxism," *left history*, 1 (Spring 1993), pp.67-102; Palmer, *Descent into Discourse: The Reification of Language and the Writing of Social History* (Philadelphia: Temple University Press, 1990).

5. For Nietzsche and Joyce see Berman, *All That Is Solid Melts into Air*. The statement by Henry Ford appeared in an interview with Charles N. Wheeler, *Chicago Tribune*, May 25, 1916.

6. Jameson, *Postmodernism*, pp.64-65.

7. I am oppositionally paraphrasing Marx's statement from "The Eighteenth Brumaire of Louis Bonaparte," in Karl Marx and Frederick Engels, *Selected Works* (Moscow: Progress, 1968), p.97: "Men make their own history, but they

do not make it just as they please." This is obviously somewhat facetious, since Goodyear did not come to Napanee "just as it pleased," having to go billions of dollars into debt to thwart a hostile takeover attempt, facing the intense competition of a restructured rubber industry, paying out millions in benefits to laid-off unionized workers, etc. etc. Yet my point is that Goodyear managed to secure itself a fairly free hand in negotiating its conquest of eastern Ontario.

8. Fredric Jameson, *The Political Unconscious: Narrative as a Socially Symbolic Act* (London: Methuen, 1983), esp. pp.9, 20.

9. Although Student Council president Mark Arsenault is now convinced that Goodyear had made its decision to locate in Napanee before the supposedly key events occurred at NDSS, what did happen was convenient. Interview with Arsenault, March 22, 1993. See, as well, *Student Assembly Video*, Dec. 11, 1987, NDSS Library. In April 1993 CBC-TV's *Venture* aired a program on the increasing relevance of education and training. The NDSS-Goodyear connection was central to the televised business program.

10. Larry Pantages, "Mercer Says Law Spurred Decision," *Akron Beacon Journal*, April 12, 1988; "Goodyear in Canada" (editorial), *Akron Beacon Journal*, April 13, 1988; "Costs of Expansion Outweighs Sales Rise," *The Financial Post Daily*, May 20, 1988.

11. The artist sketch appeared in *The Whig-Standard*, April 15, 1988, accompanying Paulette Peirol, "Site Sketches Show Streamlined Plant," while the open house statements are in Hagerman, "Goodyear Unveils Initial Plans for Plant." My assessment of the stark contrast between Goodyear's preconstruction artistic presentation of its plant and the subsequent reality has been tempered somewhat by seasonal change. The factory site is perhaps at its most drab in early spring, when I was finishing this book. Things look a little better in the lush green of early summer, but not so much that the contrast between promotion and presence disappears.

12. For suggestive accounts of an entirely different context in which pacts with the devil are more than metaphorical, see June Nash, *We Eat the Mines and the Mines Eat Us: Dependency and Exploitation in Bolivian Tin Mines* (New York: Columbia University Press, 1979); Michael Taussig, *The Devil and Commodity Fetishism in South America* (Chapel Hill: University of North Carolina Press, 1980).

13. For pro-labour discussions of the team concept, see Mike Parker and Jane Slaughter, *Choosing Sides: Unions and the Team Concept* (Boston: South End Press, 1988); Mike Parker, "Industrial Relations Myth and the Shop-Floor Reality: The 'Team Concept' in the Auto Industry," in *Industrial Democracy in America*, ed. Lichtenstein and Harris, pp.249-274.

14. For Goodyear executives' 1988 salary, bonus, and stock data, see *Akron Beacon Journal*, June 5, 1989, in DBF.